THE GREAT AGE OF FRESCO

THE GREAT AGE
OF FRESCO

Discoveries, Recoveries
and Survivals

MILLARD MEISS

George Braziller

in association with

The Metropolitan Museum of Art

NEW YORK 1970

Published in 1970
All rights reserved
No part of the contents of this book may be reproduced
without the written consent of the publisher,
George Braziller, Inc.
One Park Avenue
New York, N.Y. 10016
Standard Book Number 0-8076-0558-1
Library of Congress Catalog Card No.: 70-115985
Design by Jennie Bush
Printed by Amilcare Pizzi, Milan, Italy

CONTENTS

PREFACE

This book bears the title of an unprecedented exhibition, an exhibition that twenty years ago could not have been held even in Italy and will never again be held outside it. Great frescoes that by the very technique of execution were bound to the walls of Italian buildings have been stripped off in an extensive campaign to preserve them. Seventy of these detached frescoes and monumental drawings, most of them from Florence, were sent to the Metropolitan Museum in New York and then to a number of European cities. Everywhere these thin layers of color, shorn so to speak of their walls and then mounted on sheets of board or plastic, were greeted with surprise and wonder. They also aroused great admiration, for among them were works of the rarest beauty. They had been sent abroad less than two years after the destructive flood of 1966, Professor Procacci of Florence wrote, "as a tribute from the Italian people, especially from the city of Florence and other cities in Tuscany, to all those who contributed, and are still contributing, to the saving of a cultural and artistic patrimony of which Florence is the custodian but which belongs to the whole civilized world."

Though hundreds of thousands of people could thus enjoy Italian murals on Fifth Avenue, a far greater number from other parts of the country could not; and of those who did see the paintings some will no doubt value a record in good color. But the plates of this publication do much more than present in color what the catalogue of the exhibition offered on a smaller scale in black and white. The book reproduces, in fact, two kinds of paintings. There are first what I believe to be the most beautiful or the most interesting frescoes and *sinopie* in the exhibition. (Each one is designated in the text opposite the plate by an asterisk below the title.) The lesser works have been omitted, and I have added instead reproductions of seventy-five frescoes in Italy. In general these additions preserve the chronological and geographic range of the paintings in the exhibition; they are mostly Tuscan, or at least by Tuscan artists, and they were painted from the thirteenth through the sixteenth centuries. The Roman, North Italian and Venetian traditions, however, could not remain unrepresented, and there is an epilogue on the Baroque and the eighteenth century.

Selecting reproductions for this book was in some respects like choosing frescoes for the exhibition—a choice in which I participated as the representative of the Metropolitan Museum. In both instances it was not possible, for one reason or another, to have everything that I or, in the case of the exhibition, my Florentine colleagues wanted. The selections for the book were made over a longer period of time—five months—and commitments had to be undertaken along the way. If a few frescoes are reproduced that do not now seem to meet my final criteria of quality and condition, they all contribute something significant to our knowledge of this distinctive and magnificent art.

Though the scope of the book is thus much greater, a correspondence of another kind with the exhibition has been maintained. A few of the seventy-five additional frescoes have been recently discovered. Many of them have been detached from the wall, and almost all of them have been cleaned of the heavy layers of dirt, salts, and fixatives deposited over the centuries. Not a few of them likewise have benefited enormously from the removal of the misguided repainting of earlier restorers. The disclosure of the original colors has amounted to a spectacular recuperation. In some instances it has occurred so recently that not even all interested historians have been able to see the paintings in their new state.

This volume may serve to celebrate, then, the salvage and recovery of some of the most splendid monumental paintings in the world. Like the exhibition that inspired it the book brings close to the observer, though only in reproduction of course, frescoes that are difficult to see in their original places high on the wall and in a poor light. Since paintings of this kind are normally very large, details rather than complete paintings seemed normally more suitable to the pages of a book. In the past I have written about some of these frescoes in volumes addressed to scholars and students, and those observations that seemed useful for the present publication have been included. I have been much impressed at the same time by the greater demands of writing about paintings reproduced in good color rather than in black and white. The presence of so much more of the work of art, especially on a facing page, naturally induces hesitancy and stills talk. Good color reproduction offers great opportunities to the historian of art but it also presents a formidable challenge.

Although the evidence in the plates that follow provides an occasion for rejoicing in what has been recovered, I regret to add that my visits to dozens of churches for the purpose of selecting outstanding, well-preserved frescoes proved discouraging in one important respect. Everyone familiar with the unique riches of the Italian mural tradition would begin the preparation of a book such as this with a selection more or less different from my final one. I fear that no one, however, would readily find another set of frescoes in the same good state. Mural paintings are deteriorating at an alarming rate, partly because of un-precedented pollution of the air. Even cycles that a few years ago seemed fresh in color, such as Altichiero's in the Chapel of St. George in Padua or the *Life of St. Francis* in Assisi, now must be seen through a white film of salts. In the frescoes by Fra Filippo Lippi in the Cathedral of Prato I could not find one attractive detail that met the standards of condition I had set. The custodians of this wonderful heritage, who have already done so much to preserve it, continue to face an immense task. They need the sympathetic attention and the help of all who care, and I fervently hope this book will increase their number.

M. M.

Princeton
December, 1969

8

Oil and mud deposited by the flood in the Church of Ognissanti, Florence, below Botticelli's *St. Augustine* (see p. 170).

ACKNOWLEDGMENTS

Of the many Italian authorities who generously gave permission for photography I wish to thank first of all Ugo Procacci and his colleagues Umberto Baldini and Giuseppe Marchini in the Soprintendenza alle Gallerie in Florence, Soprintendenti Enzo Carli of Siena, Cesare Gnudi of Bologna, Francesco Valcanover of Venice, and Dr. Deoclecio Redig de Campos of the Vatican Gallery. I am grateful also to the ecclesiastical authorities at all the churches in which the frescoes are preserved.

I have learned much from discussions of technique with my friends in the Soprintendenze and among the restorers, first of all Leonetto Tintori, and also Giuseppe Rosi, Alfio del Serra and Dino Dini, all of Florence, Ottorino Nonfarmale of Bologna, and Paolo Mora of Rome. Professor H. W. Janson very kindly read the text and made a number of valuable suggestions. I owe useful observations to Professors John Plummer and Donald Weinstein.

Without the sustained interest of the publishers, George Braziller, and Thomas P. F. Hoving and Theodore Rousseau of the Metropolitan Museum, the book would not have been undertaken. It is a pleasure to acknowledge the work of the very large team that is necessary for the production of a book of this kind. I should like to thank particularly Bradford Kelleher of the Publications Department at the Metropolitan Museum; John Clark of the photographic firm of Scala in Florence, and Dr. Ileana Margarolo of the same firm; Robin Bledsoe of the house of Braziller; Mrs. Gudrun Buettner of the Chanticleer Press; Jennie Bush; the skilled craftsmen of the firm of Amilcare Pizzi in Milan. Mrs. Johanna Cornelissen flawlessly prepared and copy edited the manuscript. Mrs. Elizabeth H. Beatson participated in many aspects of the work, from the initial selection of the frescoes to the exploration of problems posed by the attempt to describe even the most familiar masterpieces.

M. M.

THE GREAT AGE OF FRESCO

INTRODUCTION

Since that day in 1786 when Goethe, arriving in Assisi on his journey to the great Italian Pages
monuments of the past, strode right by the church of San Francesco to contemplate the 39, 73
remains of a modest Roman temple, our civilization has learned to understand and to enjoy
a superb form of art. Painting before Raphael had been ignored from the later sixteenth
through the eighteenth centuries even by persons as cultivated as the great German poet. It
began to be admired in the era of Romanticism, and since then Italian frescoes, early as well as
late, have been recognized as a central part of our artistic heritage. The monumental murals
that survive suggest to us the dazzling appearance of Italy during the late Middle Ages
and the Renaissance. Contemporary descriptions prove that the walls of countless churches,
public buildings and great houses shone with murals that told the traditional Christian stories
and the recently revived Greek myths. Nor did one see such a display only indoors. Everywhere
in Central Italy, in the Veneto and in the valley of the Po façades bore frescoes, insufficiently
protected from the weather and practically all lost today. Across the piazza from the Cathedral
of Siena stories of the life of the Virgin adorned the façade of the Hospital. The countryside, too, did not lack art of this kind; frescoed tabernacles rose at innumerable crossroads. 157

This glorious wealth of monumental painting, unmatched at any other time in history,
could have been produced only by a passion for the art that was widely diffused through
society. Patrons in great numbers, whether public or private, generally chose their painters
well; we know of no exceptional artist who failed to win major commissions. Occasionally
a lesser master was invited to undertake important work—for example I at least, unlike
Piero de'Medici, would not have chosen Benozzo Gozzoli to paint the chapel of my palace.
Still, the level of performance was astonishingly high.

All this activity coincided with the rapid growth of the Italian city-states and the no
less rapid spread of the new mendicant orders. The meeting halls of town councils acquired
murals that invoked the support of Christ, the Virgin and local saints, or that offered to the 141,
rulers models of piety, moral strength, mercy, and wisdom. The city fathers sometimes 79, 206
honored successful military generals with monuments that simulated stone in paint, and they 125
condemned what they considered internal enemies of the state by engaging masters such as
Castagno and Sarto to display them in fresco on the façade of a municipal building, dangling
by their feet. Nor were these varied enterprises limited to the republics. In the halls of fortified
palaces the North Italian despots celebrated their authority and their triumphs in cycles 160, 166
that were often artistically memorable. The Dominicans and especially the Franciscans,
who strove to engage the populace by delivering sermons in the vernacular rather than in
Latin, commissioned what might be called sermons in paint on the walls of their new 25

churches. For their own contemplation the friars commonly had the Last Supper represented on a wall of the refectory in which they ate. Wealthy merchants erected or bought chapels in these churches and covered their walls with stories of their patron saints. Occasionally a very rich man, such as Enrico Scrovegni of Padua, built an independent chapel and had it adorned with murals. Pope Sixtus IV and his successors created a monument of this kind on a grand scale in the Sistine Chapel. Archbishops, too, adorned their palaces with impressive pictorial cycles. Men of more limited means chose fresco as a good and cheap substitute for sculpture, even having their tombs painted rather than carved. To give church interiors a greater unity altarpieces or paintings just above altars were occasionally executed in fresco rather than on panel.

54, 62

43

176, 210,

230

65

68

Of all this splendor we possess only a small part today, and that thanks to the relative stability of Italian civilization and especially of the Church. The three centuries beginning in 1500 no longer understood or valued the art of the preceding period, but it was nevertheless frequently respected, largely for religious reasons. Later Italians, furthermore, did not entirely forget the conviction held by their predecessors from the fourteenth century on that their art was novel, precious, and enormously important. The Italians of the Renaissance proudly traced the origin of their culture in general to the ancient Romans, and, though they did not mention it, their practice of fresco owed much to these ancestors also. The Romans of antiquity, like earlier Mediterranean peoples, enjoyed large mural paintings in their palaces and villas. As we know from surviving buildings in Rome and the region of Pompeii, they transformed confining walls into large, fictive spaces. They converted stone, brick and plaster into gardens and fanciful architecture. Mural paintings also brought near the adventures of the gods and the practices of religious cults. For all these purposes the Romans employed a variety of pictorial techniques, among them a kind of fresco. It was described as early as the first century B.C. by Vitruvius in his famous treatise on architecture, which was well known to later Italian artists and scholars.

26

29

The Italian word *fresco* means fresh, and a fresco is made by applying pigments mixed with water to freshly spread, damp plaster. Some pigments cannot be applied in water without soon undergoing chemical change—the widely used azurite blue, for instance, turns green. These pigments must therefore be mixed with a binder and painted on dry plaster, a technique known by the Italian word for dry, *secco*. Thus, because of the special requirements of such pigments, for which no practical substitute was known, murals executed entirely in fresco are extremely rare. Fresco was, however, the technique most highly prized from 1300 to 1450, and it was still employed in a more or less modified form for several centuries afterward. It has a peculiar and very important property: when the wet plaster made of slaked lime dries, the carbonation that occurs binds the pigments into a solid crystalline mass. These crystals are reflective and highly durable unless subjected to moisture combined with chemicals in the wall or in the modern polluted air.

85

Fresco paintings thus retain to an exceptional degree their original colors. This important advantage was emphasized by the first great historian of art, Giorgio Vasari. In an enthusiastic account published in 1550 Vasari praised the durability and the brightness of fresco and called it the most beautiful of pictorial techniques. He warned against executing part of the surface *a secco*, because, he said, the colors would appear less luminous and would gradually darken. We know that paintings made with an oil vehicle slowly darken also.

Among the paintings that have come down to us from the past, therefore, frescoes are exceptional in an important respect. Many of the colors are quite unaltered. Unlike paintings in oil and some in tempera, furthermore, frescoes were never coated with glazes or colored varnish. They bore no film of any kind. When they are cleaned, therefore, there is no risk of disturbing extremely thin, easily dissolved coatings. The removal when possible of dirt, repaint, fixatives, or of oil spread in the vain hope of brightening the surfaces, simply reveals to us once again the original colors in all their limpid beauty. Properly cleaned frescoes are entirely valid documents of the taste of their time, and they are therefore relevant to the problem of cleaning panels and canvases that has been studied and vigorously debated in recent years. Of course, painters sought a somewhat different coloristic effect in fresco than in tempera or in oil. But no one who has seen the recently recovered surfaces of Botticelli's frescoes in the Vatican or of Filippino's in S. Maria Novella, examples of which are 176, 181 reproduced in this book, can ever look again in quite the same way at the many darkened, yellow and greenish panels and canvases of these artists.

The durability of fresco was a quality highly valued in an age of religious art; the church was the house of a timeless God. An *appearance* of permanence, indeed, was as important as actual durability. Altarpieces of the time were painted on solid wood. There was available, to be sure, a beautiful mural technique—glass mosaic—that offered still greater durability than fresco. It was largely invented in the Early Christian period, and it was often used in Italy during the Middle Ages, particularly by patrons possessing large resources, 31 kings, emperors, popes and members of their entourage. Mosaics, however, were costly and the execution was slow, characteristics that did not recommend themselves to the new bourgeois patrons of art. The technique, furthermore, served best a certain mode or style; it was admirably suited to large, relatively flat and rigid forms. The innumerable small vari-colored cubes, each tilted at a slightly different angle, acted as reflectors of light and they produced marvelously luminous images. The composition of forms by the use of glass cubes did not, however, lend itself to the more realistic art of the late Middle Ages and the Renaissance.

Stained glass, a medieval technique related to mosaic, was found to have similar disadvantages in the fourteenth and later centuries. This glorious method of transforming 25 natural light, so as to "urge us onward," Abbot Suger of St. Denis said about 1145, "from the material to the immaterial," was more widely used in Italy than is generally supposed. It attained its greatest results earlier, however, in the twelfth and thirteenth centuries, and in Northern Europe, especially France. Specific shapes and stories are less distinguishable in glass, so that in Italy the mendicant friars, at least, must have found its didactic possibilities limited. Like fresco, stained glass was built up from patches, the outlines of which frequently coincided with the contours of the main forms. The patches of glass, however, were far smaller, and their metal framework, which necessarily remained quite visible, interfered with the creation of monumental forms and of spatial illusion.

When in 1550 Giorgio Vasari wrote in praise of fresco it was no longer widely practiced and it therefore required, he believed, defense and championship. It is, he said, the most beautiful of all pictorial techniques, and also the most difficult. It is difficult, for one thing, because wet colors look quite different after they have dried, so that the painter needs great experience to know what final effects he is producing. Fresco is difficult also because the fresh plaster dries rapidly and the painter had to work fast. Indeed, he spread only as much plaster as he could paint in a day. For a mural executed *a secco*, the normal medieval technique, the plaster was laid before painting in large horizontal bands (see diagram opposite). A picture executed in fresco, on the other hand, consists of a series of irregular patches painted on successive days, as the illustrations on pages 19 and 35 show. Only those colors, chiefly blues, that had to be applied in a non-aqueous vehicle could be added at leisure, any time after the plaster had dried.

True fresco was exacting in still another respect. To understand how, we must consider other peculiarities of the technique. The upper layer of plaster (called *intonaco*) that was spread for the daily task of painting was fine-grained and thin. The shape of the patch was irregular because it was governed in part by a wish to include all of an area of comparatively uniform color. The patch of *intonaco* was laid over a much coarser and thicker layer of plaster called the *arriccio*. Now it was on this first coarse layer that the painter, from about 1250 to 1450, normally drew in full scale the figures and other important forms as a guide for what he intended to paint. For these preliminary drawings he used a red pigment called *sinopia*.

It is one of the peculiarities of fresco that the daily patch of fine plaster concealed precisely the part of the drawing that the master was about to paint. When all the patches were spread the drawing was of course entirely hidden. The modern process of detaching frescoes (at least the *stacco* method) to a degree reverses the process of execution, peeling the *intonaco* away from the *arriccio* and disclosing the *sinopia*, as the accompanying reproduction shows.

The rapid painting of a form without benefit of a corresponding, continuously visible full-scale drawing was appropriate only to a period in which forms were relatively conventional. All heads, for example, approximated canons to such a degree that the singularities of each could be remembered or invented as the artist quickly painted without a drawing before him. About 1450 the increasing individuality, life-likeness, and therefore uniqueness of forms brought two basic changes in technique, one affecting the preparatory drawing, the other the nature of the painting. Artists began to make full-scale drawings of the important forms on paper or cloth; they prepared them beforehand, and then transferred them to the wall, normally to the *intonaco*. At first they usually effected the transfer by pricking holes along the lines of the cartoon, pressing it against the *intonaco*, and dusting

143

152

Design of patches of *intonaco* for painting *a secco*. Roman Painter, ca. 1290, *Creation of Eve*, Assisi, San Francesco, Upper Church (see p. 37).

A fresco, faced with cloth, and its *intonaco* are rolled away from the *arriccio*, on which the *sinopia* drawing becomes visible.

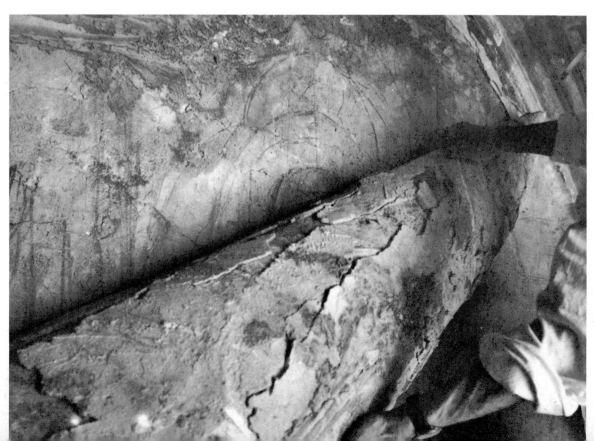

charcoal or another pigment through these holes. Soon painters preferred to run a stylus over the lines as the cartoon was held against the damp *intonaco*, into which they thus made incisions.

57

134–143

The full-scale drawing or cartoon recorded on the final surface the relatively individual form, whereas the earlier *sinopia* recorded on the preliminary surface the comparatively canonical form. The individualized forms of the mid-fifteenth century required more time to realize in paint also, and masters such as Piero della Francesca began to free themselves of the tyranny of the daily fresco patch. Since to gain time they were forced to rely less on the adhesion obtained by the carbonation of the lime they added organic binders to their vehicle. Thus they could work on less moist *intonaco*, and their technique approached (without however equaling) *secco*.

144

The patches in a fresco always succeeded one another from the top down, as in the *Dream of Constantine* in Arezzo by Piero della Francesca, a diagram of which is here reproduced. This succession downward avoided spilling paint on a newly executed patch, and it permitted a regular lowering of the scaffold as the work progressed. Usually the patches were laid also from left to right. Thus the painter was not free to proceed, as he would be in other techniques, from an important central area out toward the margins of the composition. For the fresco of the *Dream*, which is about ten feet high, Piero first set his scaffold a couple of feet below the lower edge of patch 3. Then he painted the rest of the composition from a platform below the lower frame.

It is clear, then, that as the artist moved down the wall his forms normally came forward in the illusory space. Such a procedure demanded that at the outset the painter envisage clearly the entire fresco, especially because changes were so difficult to make. When Piero painted the upper parts of the tents or the soldiers he needed to have very vividly in mind what was to follow below. In the instance of the *Dream*, which is somewhat unusual, the progression from deep space to foreground was not regular. From the angel in patch 2, painted after the strip of sky in 1, Piero retreated in space to the tents. Similarly from the soldier in patches 4 and 5 he moved back to the watcher in 6 and 7. These journeys in and out of space notwithstanding, he had to get everything right the first time. He could correct mistakes only by knocking out the *intonaco* and applying a fresh patch.

144

The very design of Piero's patches indicates that he was employing the new version of the fresco technique to which I referred above. Earlier masters had avoided executing an area of continuous color on two patches; otherwise they ran the risk of a failure to match because of the great difficulty of predicting how wet colors would look when dry. The number and irregular shapes of Piero's patches prove that he wished to paint on damp plaster, but in three instances he permitted a color to fall into two patches: the wing of the angel, the post of the tent, and the seated watcher. In two of these instances he avoided problems of matching by adopting a new procedure. In the wing and the post the final strokes of his brush carried over the joints separating the patches. Piero evidently employed devices to keep his plaster damp for longer periods. For this purpose he apparently used

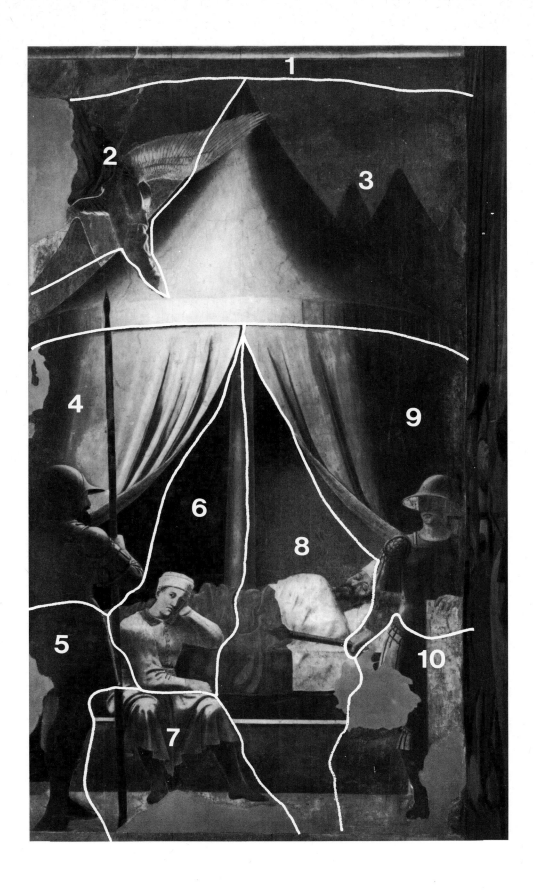

Piero della Francesca, *Dream of Constantine*, Cathedral, Arezzo. Ten patches of *intonaco* on which the fresco was painted.

wet cloth; one may still see here and there its imprint in the *intonaco*. More important, he included an adhesive in his vehicle so that he could continue to paint on drier, or even entirely dried, plaster.

Mural techniques related to Piero's became more common than true fresco in the centuries following. Painters even worked on entirely dry walls; Padre Pozzo, writing in 1700, said this *secco* technique was frequently employed in Rome. In the seventeenth and eighteenth centuries, furthermore, the problem of the adhesion of the pigments to drying plaster could be met in a new way. Sand was added to the surface to make it rougher and more binding. This technical change was again linked with a stylistic one, because at this time forms were realized by a very open brushwork. Earlier, when forms were more precisely finished and brushstrokes proportionately small, painters insisted upon an *intonaco* that was very smooth.

During the fourteenth and fifteenth centuries the bright colors of frescoed walls were approximated in altarpieces and other panels by a tempera technique that used an egg vehicle. In the late fifteenth century, however, leading masters such as Leonardo da Vinci and Giovanni Bellini accelerated the trend toward new pictorial effects by painting in oil. This innovation was accompanied, particularly in Venice, by the adoption of canvas. Cloth offered many advantages: it permitted any size, providing even very large surfaces; it was comparatively light and could be more readily transported, allowing the painter to produce his work in a studio. Canvases replaced not only altar panels but also frescoes, again especially in Venice.

Murals too began to be painted in oil on dry plaster. Oil dries much more slowly than water or egg, and it therefore gave the painter freedom to alter and rework. On the wall the possibility of making changes was especially advantageous, because they were so difficult to accomplish in fresco. Oil also offered a lustrous surface, a new range of deep colors, and a greater capacity to realize evanescent spatial and psychological depths.

Of course the novel possibilities offered by the oil technique were obtained only by sacrificing other qualities. To Michelangelo these losses appeared very great. When he learned that the huge altar wall of the Sistine Chapel had been completely plastered at the pope's command so that he could paint the Last Judgment on it in oil, he gave orders to destroy the thoroughly dry *intonaco* and proceeded to work in fresco. As a viscous material with some color, oil altered the quality of the plaster far more than fresco had. This difference is fundamental, because one of the most beautiful properties of true fresco is its conformity with the wall. It conforms in fact as well as in appearance because a fresco is, as we have seen, physically and chemically a part of the wall. Furthermore, lime plaster, with which the pigments become united, is an architectural material. Frescoes therefore preserve the character and function of the wall. They maintain its plane, which is usually flat, but they can equally well follow the curve of the wall into vaults, apses, and domes. More than any other kind of painting the crystalline layer of fresco resembles the basic materials of building—plaster, mortar and stone.

While offering these special possibilities, the fresco technique does not exclude different, even paradoxical, effects. Frescoes that seem to be part of the wall may at the same time create illusory projections in front of or behind it. The force and degree of these projections generally increase from the fourteenth century on, in conformity with the development of pictorial and architectural styles. Because the several arts at a given time always shared certain qualities, the relationship between frescoes and the building that contains them was most intimate when they covered the walls of a contemporary structure. Indeed many buildings or at least rooms were designed to receive frescoes. This was true not only of churches, such as S. Francesco at Assisi and the Arena Chapel in Padua, but also of monumental cemeteries such as the Camposanto at Pisa, of town halls, as at Siena, and of private dwellings, such as Villa Maser. However, it must be said that a number of great architects of the Renaissance, above all Brunelleschi and Alberti, like Frank Lloyd Wright and Mies van der Rohe in our time, disliked having the surfaces of their buildings altered by monumental paintings conceived by others. In his influential treatise on architecture written in the middle of the fifteenth century, Alberti relegated murals to the forecourt of a church. For the interior he preferred panels to murals and, indeed, statues to panels.

67
209
118
43
89, 79
219

Frescoes may add simulated sculptures to a building. They may also complete or even extend its structure, or they may partially transform it, creating a rich and fascinating interplay between the real and the almost-real. In 1866 the great French critic Hippolyte Taine, writing of Raphael's *Liberation of St. Peter*, remarked that the fresco is not isolated: in composition and character, he said, it is the complement of the window below it. The frescoed walls of S. Croce in Florence and the later cloister by Andrea del Sarto impress upon us the deep connection between the constant practice of fresco and the persistent nature of Italian pictorial style. The scale of frescoes, their architectural character, and their large audience seem to call forth an orderly, rational, geometric art. Or we might reverse the causal relationship and say that this kind of artistic taste and purpose produced the enduring vogue for monumental frescoes. In any event a similar taste and practice existed already in ancient Rome.

225
219
192
25
198
26

The Italians, with their special feeling for plasticity and for stone, preferred paintings that were identified with, or even a function of, the wall. Diaphanous glass, appearing precisely where the wall does not, remained a secondary art in the peninsula. The glowing interiors of Northern cathedrals were never matched in Italy, not even in the seventeenth century, which exploited effects of light. Though Renaissance Italians admired the deep color of stained glass windows they preferred frescoes that told clearly stories of saints and, later, of pagan gods, and that displayed on a grand scale the great events in man's religious history.

25

ITALY
Locations of the Frescoes

THE PLATES AND LEGENDS

An asterisk (*) below the title of a legend designates a painting shown in the exhibition The Great Age of Fresco.

TRANSEPT AND APSE, SANTA CROCE, FLORENCE

Architecture, Painting and Glass, Fourteenth Century

The nave of Santa Croce—the largest in Europe between Emperor Constantine's St. Peter's and the existing building that replaced it—ends in this vast display of images in color, overall about ninety feet high. The windows, glowing with an eastern light, are more radiant than the frescoes. The stained glass, like huge precious stones, transforms the structure into a great jewelled reliquary. It is, however, the painted crucifix and the frescoes that at a distance present distinct figures and readable stories. The large scenes at the sides of the choir begin to be distinguishable as representations of the Assumption of the Virgin and the Stigmatization of St. Francis even near the main entrance to the church, more than three hundred feet away.

When planning the building the friars and their architect no doubt intended such large, flat walls for frescoes. Giotto, the painter of the *Stigmatization*, departed from the traditional representation of this event by turning the saint from profile toward the beholder, creating a monumental, emblematic image at a focal point of the entire church. A similar square field on the opposite side of the choir is devoted to the *Assumption of the Virgin* by the Master of the Fogg *Pietà*, which maintains the same large scale and clarity.

Frescoes flow from such large fields as these onto the structural members and into every crevice of the building. The great piers of the choir, still identifiable as such, rest on fictive marble bases, which in turn support tabernacles occupied by saints—all products of the painter's brush. The movement upward that the piers and their frescoes engender is continued toward the roof by simulated spiral columns. The painter has invited us to join an engaging game of make-believe, in which we do not immediately discover where the building ends and the fresco begins.

A religious program governs all the representations; they center on the Cross, to which the church is dedicated. The great intercessor, the Virgin Mary, appears at the left; the founder of the order, St. Francis, at the right. Above the chancel are Old Testament prophets with scrolls who foretell Christ's coming. Within the fictive niches stand saints bearing crosses. Inside the choir, in frescoes and in glass, appear the members of the Christian hierarchy and stories of the history of the Cross.

ROMAN, MID-FIRST CENTURY B.C., MURAL PAINTING   Detail

New York, Metropolitan Museum of Art, Bedroom from Villa at Boscoreale

Lava is a more benign destructive agent than many made by man; when it buries it preserves. Everyone knows that most of the ancient Roman paintings we have were found on the walls of houses in the seaside town of Pompeii, which disappeared in the eruption of Vesuvius in A.D. 79. Excavation at Pompeii began in the eighteenth century, but the villa at Boscoreale, about a mile from the city, was found only in 1900. The mural paintings that came to light in a bedroom are unique, for they emerged almost completely preserved, and very few other Roman paintings equal them in beauty.

The room, one of the smaller spaces in a large villa, is about thirteen feet wide and thirty feet long, and the painting reproduced is the first of three compartments that one sees on the left wall upon entering. In the architectural structure that is created entirely by painting a marble base runs around the room, and an entablature at the ceiling is supported by piers and columns. The red marble columns, which rise from golden acanthus leaves and are entwined by golden arabesques, surpass in splendor any actual columns that survive.

The dramatic mask of a satyr with gaping mouth and staring eyes faces toward the right, and all the forms in the three compartments are intended to be seen from a position near the center of the wall, where there is a shrine somewhat deeper in the illusory space — the recession to it is visible at the right in the reproduction. The unified perspective of the entire wall is accompanied by a unity of light. The right-hand sides of all buildings are bright, and all cast shadows fall to the left. This system corresponds with the actual source of light in the room—a window to the right of this wall.

Above the base there rises the most imposing architectural view in ancient painting. The buildings tower behind an enclosing wall and a luxurious portal, inlaid with tortoise-shell and studded with silver ornaments. To the right of it stand a cylindrical altar, on which a fire burns, and a column that supports a statue of a female divinity, who holds two smoking torches.

For a long time this magnificent portal and the buildings behind it were believed to represent part of the theatrical setting for a comedy, as described by the contemporary architect Vitruvius. Most scholars now find here instead an ideal villa. The towers immediately behind the enclosure are farm buildings. The arched openings serve as pigeon lofts; the door above the ladder opens onto a granary. The more distant colonnaded structures, one a huge portico, the other temple-like, presumably served for repose, contemplation, and prayer.

It was to a similar but less splendid building and farm that the owner of the villa at Boscoreale, like many other wealthy Romans, retreated from the taxing life of the great city. There, in the words of Virgil, "they enjoyed repose without care, and a life that knows no fraud, but is rich in treasures manifold."

27

ROMAN, *ca.* 38 B.C., MURAL PAINTING   Detail

Rome, Museo delle Terme, from Villa of Livia

These beautiful paintings came from a partly subterranean room in a garden house built for Livia, the wife of Emperor Augustus, at Prima Porta on the Via Flaminia about nine miles from Rome. They were executed only some ten years later than the murals from Boscoreale, but they differ from that and other ancient cycles by lacking an architectural framework. Entering the room, one sees no columns, piers, and entablature, but only a small painted fringe along the vault above and a low yellow trellis and pink stone wall that bound a path that winds around the room.

A few plants grow at the far side of the path in front of the wall, and beyond it we see a profusion of flowers, bushes, and trees that is unique in ancient painting. So thick are the plants that one can see through the tangle only to a limited depth. All this lush flora grows freely, assuming unique and often surprising shapes. Though the same species are repeated, no two leaves are alike. Occasionally, as in the reproduction, a small branch hangs over the wall.

In the area of the wall reproduced a pomegranate tree stands amidst laurel, oleander, and cypress. The long slender branches are weighed down by the ripening fruit. The wonderful vitality of the scene is increased by the birds, which are painted with equal skill and affection. A blackbird flies toward the pomegranates; a handsome violet, blue and black jay turns its bill toward a yellow arbutus berry; and a red-legged partridge stands in the foliage below. All of this seems in perfect accord with the dictum of Vitruvius in a book dedicated to the Emperor Augustus: "Pictures cannot be approved that do not resemble reality."

The pomegranates perhaps refer to Proserpina, daughter of Jupiter. The god decreed that after her abduction into the underworld by Pluto, she could return only if she had eaten nothing while there. Since she had tasted some pomegranate seeds Jupiter condemned her to spend half of each year in the underworld. He permitted her to ascend from it only during the other six months, including the season represented in the painting, summer.

BYZANTINE, MID-SIXTH CENTURY, GABRIEL

Ravenna, Sant' Apollinare in Classe, Apse

On the narrow wall just outside the apse of the church the archangel stands on guard. The term is not inappropriate because Byzantine art even near its beginning associated the transcendent Christian mysteries with the ceremonial of the imperial court. Gabriel's gorgeous dress, his gold and purple mantle, fastened with a great jewel at his shoulder, and his shoes glistening with gems, all resemble the dress of the Emperor Justinian himself in a mosaic of the nearby church of S. Vitale. Actually the two churches, one in the city, the other in the port (Classe), were consecrated in the same year. The same wealthy banker financed them, and the mosaics at Classe were influenced by those of S. Vitale.

Though Gabriel is given a platform on which to stand he tends, despite his bulk, to remain suspended in the shining gold that surrounds him. The medium of mosaic can express perfectly such conceptions of partly immaterial splendor. Gabriel's wide staring eyes are shifted toward the left, so that they look in the direction of a visitor approaching the apse and the altar within it. This is the sanctuary of the church, and the words written in Greek on the angel's sacred military standard or *labarum* refer to it: Holy, Holy, Holy. These words also introduce the canon of the Mass.

The mosaic curves with the wall into the apse; a string of precious stones decorates the axis of the turn. A similar string marks the turn into the window, where a fictive column supports a fanciful arch consisting of a meandering ribbon. The space between the windows ("painted" somewhat later) is filled with a simulated niche, the curtains of which are drawn to reveal an archbishop of Ravenna. Above, in the green flowery field, three of the twelve sheep of the dome are visible. They have been interpreted as the apostles or sometimes as the congregation of the patron saint, Apollinaris.

As in the other mosaics in Ravenna from the time of Justinian, each of the tesserae in the gold ground is tilted forward. Presumably the artists wished to direct the light from the windows above toward the worshippers below. Part of the mosaic was restored in the early years of this century. No one will have any difficulty in detecting the dull modern areas, all along the right side: the upper right area of gold, the lower right corner of the purple mantle, and the right half of the platform.

GABRIEL

PISTOIESE MASTER, *ca.* 1250, CRUCIFIXION

Detail opposite

Sinopia and diagram overleaf

Pistoia, San Domenico, Chapter House

★

This early fresco, discovered beneath whitewash some thirty years ago, was detached in 1968 to prevent further deterioration. The removal from the damp wall, accomplished by techniques developed in Florence after the great flood, disclosed a magnificent drawing, reproduced overleaf. It is not only the finest *sinopia* we have from the thirteenth century but also the earliest. Indeed until a decade ago historians believed that the true fresco and *sinopia* technique was introduced only about half a century later.

The painting was executed, as the diagram following shows, on six patches of *intonaco*. To assure the adherence of these patches the *arriccio* was scored, as one can see—a practice that was soon to be abandoned. The small patches of green, red, and blue in the border at the right are trials of color made by the painter as he proceeded with the fresco.

The drawing was executed first in ocher and then in *sinopia*. This procedure conforms with the recommendations of the earliest manual on fresco technique, written by Cennino Cennini about 1400. As usual in *sinopie* the setting is only summarily indicated. When he had completed the drawing the painter marked out, in a paler red, some changes that then appeared in the fresco. The large circle around St. John's halo, for instance, becomes in the fresco the halo of the Virgin. This is part of the basic transformation that eliminated the centurion and replaced him with John at the right of the cross. This gain in symmetry, with Christ lamented by two persons very close to him, entailed the loss of the idea of conversion, which would seem appropriate to a Dominican chapter house. The touching exchange of sorrow by the Virgin and St. John in the *sinopia* was replaced by isolated and more conventional mourning, even though the gestures of the Virgin were only slightly changed. The angels grieve with much greater abandon, each in a different way and with an intensity of emotion rarely equaled in later art.

The detail of the painting that is here reproduced was recently cleaned. All the color was applied in fresco except the dark blue in the background and the blue that the master spread *a secco* over a dark red and black fresco preparation in the dress of the Virgin. The deep, glowing color, resembling Gothic stained glass, was soon to be abandoned for lighter tones.

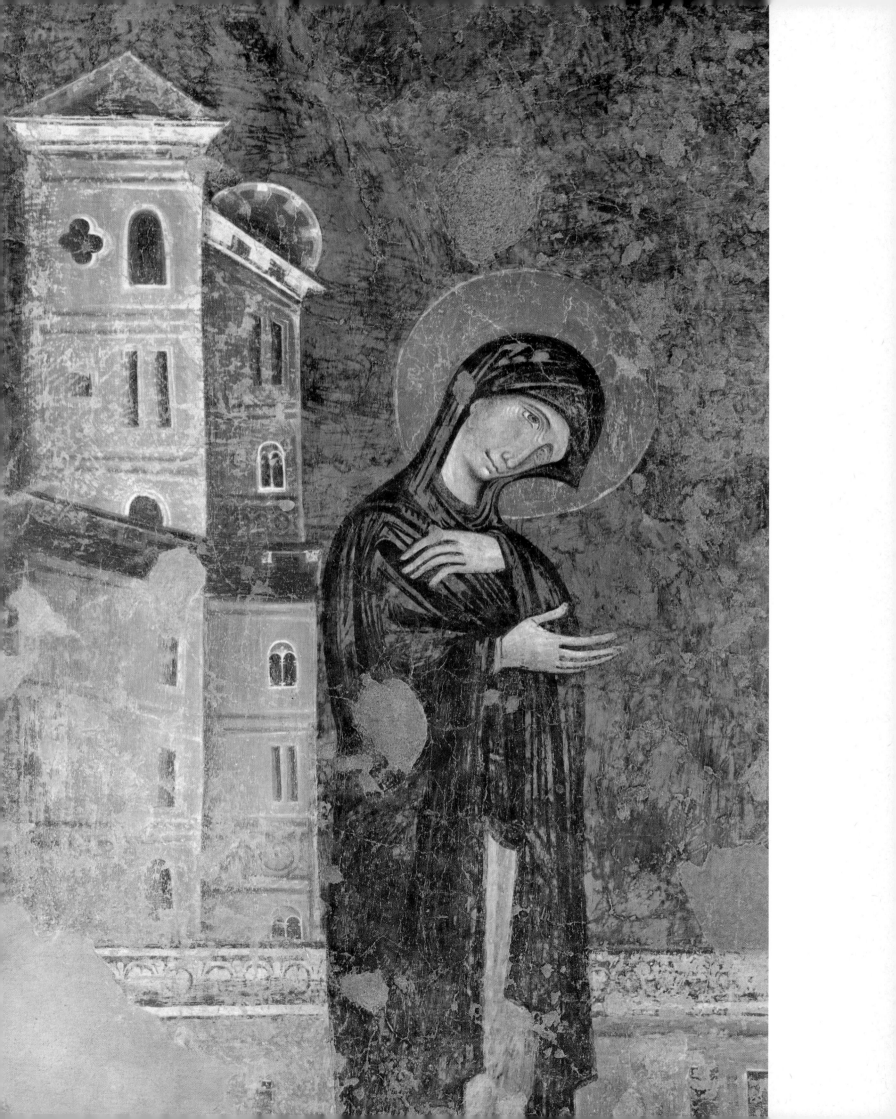

Sinopia.

34

Fresco painted on six patches of *intonaco*, one each day.

ROMAN PAINTER, *ca.* 1290, CREATION OF EVE

Assisi, San Francesco, Upper Church

On this and the following plate are reproduced two scenes from the momentous cycle of Old Testament scenes at Assisi—momentous because in it the two great styles of late-thirteenth-century painting, created by Cimabue and Cavallini, meet and merge, and out of the fusion rises Giotto. The New Testament cycle on the opposite or south wall is arranged similarly, with two rows of scenes under the vaults, and it shows a similar development, but less clearly. The painting of both walls proceeded from the crossing to the façade. The *Creation of Eve* is in the second bay from the crossing, and *Isaac and Esau* (on the following plate) is in the third.

The great difference of style between these two paintings is accompanied by a basic difference of technique. Whereas the slightly later scene of Isaac was executed in fresco, the *Creation of Eve* was painted in a technique that was commonly employed during the Middle Ages, both in Europe and the Byzantine region. The *intonaco* of the *Creation*, exclusive of the triangle just under the vault, was laid in three large bands, as the diagram on page 17 shows. The height of each band was determined by the area the plasterer and the painter could cover from one platform. Probably the artist executed some of the underpainting on each of these bands while the plaster was still damp. If it had dried he might have moistened it to obtain some carbonation, and for the same purpose he added lime to the water with which he mixed his pigments. The painting was completed *a secco*.

Inasmuch as the *Creation of Eve* is very near the *Isaac and Esau*, the visitor to the church and the reader of this book have an opportunity to compare the more opaque colors of a characteristic medieval technique with the brighter and more transparent ones painted largely in true fresco. Different in their original effect, they also deteriorate somewhat differently. This difference can be measured the more readily because the two paintings have been subjected to approximately the same destructive agents. In this comparison the crowns of the two trees should be disregarded, because a related transformation of original green sometimes occurs in paintings executed otherwise in fresco.

The arch, the vault, and the ribs still preserve their superb original decoration. The simulated brown and white brackets, deriving from an ancient Italian tradition, are early examples of what we shall find to be a continually growing use of fresco for illusionistic purposes.

GIOTTO (?), *ca.* 1292, ESAU SEEKING ISAAC'S BLESSING

Assisi, San Francesco, Upper Church

Until the technique of the Pistoia *Crucifixion* was identified (page 32), this was one of the earliest frescoes we knew.

So clear is the design of the painting and so expressive its narrative that large losses and abrasion have not obscured its dramatic power. In the preceding fresco Rebekah, taking disgraceful advantage of Isaac's blindness, has obtained his blessing for Jacob, the son she prefers, but now the older boy, Esau, comes to his father's bedside, offering the bowl of meat (and a spoon) that he had earlier been invited to bring. (The now headless figure in blue may be Jacob, eavesdropping.) The old man, surprised, gropes with one hand. The folds of the drapery swirl in response to his agitation. The woman, perhaps Rebekah or a member of the household, peers intently at Isaac, and with a beautiful gesture that suggests fear and self-defense she presses a pitcher to her bosom. The arms of Esau, though close to his father's, move in the opposite direction, and he stares into the distance—in spirit the two will never meet.

The gestures of the figures are impulsive yet sustained. Though they are in part opposed they join in a larger harmony, which is echoed by the bed-cover and the drapery. The rectangles of the tall, open building contain, stabilize, and somehow ennoble the action. This is the first painting since antiquity in which glances are focused to this degree and given so fundamental a role in the structure and content of a narrative.

In these and other respects the fresco marks a great turn in Western painting and leads directly into the art we call Renaissance. It is therefore of the utmost interest that the painter had no doubt previously worked in Rome, and that he must have been deeply impressed by the Early Christian mural cycles in the great Roman basilicas, all of which are lost today.

The Assisi fresco shares basic qualities of design and of narrative with documented paintings by Giotto, four of which are reproduced on pages 44 through 51. So deep is the resemblance that if the Isaac scene was not painted by Giotto (I believe it very probably was) its author must at least be ranked with him as a co-founder of modern painting.

Even the painter's choice of the moment in the story suggests the same conclusion. He has shown neither Isaac's initial rejection of Esau nor his ultimate halfhearted blessing, the two actions that were normally represented earlier. Instead he chose a prior moment when, according to Genesis, "Isaac his father said unto Esau, who art thou? And Esau said I am thy son, thy first-born. And Isaac trembled very exceedingly." The artist has foregone episodes in which actions are finally resolved for a moment of surprise, discovery, and maximum suspense. He cares far more about the quality of human thought and feeling than about ecclesiastical dogma.

GIOTTO OR A CONTEMPORARY, ST. FRANCIS SUPPORTING
THE LATERAN BASILICA Detail

Assisi, San Francesco, Upper Church

In 1209 the youthful friar Francis went to Rome to obtain from Pope Innocent III approval of his new order. At first the Pope remained uncertain, but then in a dream he saw the great Lateran Church of St. John begin to fall. Suddenly a man came to its support and held it up with his own body. The painter, depicting the event almost a century later, has shown St. Francis and the church in the left half of his fresco while the Pope, attended by two guards, lies asleep at the right.

In earlier medieval art miracles of this kind were represented by symbolic action. The rapidly developing realism of art around 1300, with its concern for a vivid space filled with solid, weighty forms, required a different way of telling the story. An organically articulated Francis must exert himself to check the fall of a toppling building. He becomes a caryatid, taking the place of a column and bracing himself by putting one hand on his hip and stretching a leg backward at an angle. Of course the realism is not consistent, for a building could not collapse in this manner and the proportionately over-size saint, placed within its porch, would actually fall with it. Yet if we accept the conventions of representation of the period the narrative is very impressive. Though the Saint has a massive and powerful body he looks to heaven in acknowledgment of the divine force that is ultimately responsible for his success.

The gold has come away from the halo, the white lead used in the foot and in the shaded part of the tunic has oxidized and turned dark, and the entire original surface has been lost in the upper left corner of the detail. Most of the rest, painted in true fresco, is very well preserved. The figure is also one of the most beautiful in the twenty-eight scenes of this famous cycle devoted to the legend of the Saint. Although most scholars believe that figures such as this were painted by Giotto, others, including the writer, ascribe them to a contemporary Roman master influenced by him.

GIOTTO, *ca.* 1303–1305, FRESCOES

Padua, Arena Chapel (view from chancel toward entrance)

There are in Italy or indeed in the world only a few completely painted interiors comparable to the Arena Chapel, and we almost lost it during the last war, when bombs exploded a hundred feet away. Now the frescoes are being slowly but steadily damaged by the noxious fumes of a rapidly growing local industry.

All over Europe the thirteenth century saw the development of a magnificent architecture in which the function of support was concentrated more and more in piers, columns, and ribs, while the walls between these members became diaphanous, shrank in size, and were increasingly replaced by stained glass. The Italians applied these Gothic principles only with important modifications, but even in Italy the Arena Chapel is remarkable for its lack of Gothic structure. In the Chapel round arches are generally preferred to pointed, the walls curve into the barrel vault, and apart from a few windows the smooth flat surfaces lack architectural articulation entirely. That structure Giotto supplied with his brush, in accordance with a decision probably made before the simple building took shape. Giotto was admirably qualified for such an all-encompassing task, especially because he had studied related murals of the Early Christian period, and their later echoes, in Rome.

In the lower zone of the walls Giotto introduced a dado of simulated marble panels, punctuated at left and right by simulated statues of the Virtues and Vices. In the process of painting the marble here and in the scenes above he introduced veins of color and let them spread by chance into the surrounding gray-white areas. The diffusion of this color was then promoted when he ran a hot iron over the surface, giving it the brilliance and smoothness of actual polished marble. This technique resembles one employed by the ancient Romans; whether Giotto learned it from books or by examples we do not yet know.

The marble of the dado is repeated in the buildings represented in the three rows of scenes. The backgrounds of the scenes introduce large areas of blue, a color which then spreads over the entire vault. There, strewn with golden stars, it symbolizes heaven, the abode of Christ, the Virgin and the saints who appear in golden roundels. The regular gradation of the color, from white and gray to blue and gold, is one aspect of the wonderful unity of fresco, wall and building. This unity is enhanced by the fictive arches that run across the ceiling and by the curve of the uppermost scenes, which follow the wall into the vault.

On the inside of the entrance wall, which is about forty feet high, Giotto painted, in accordance with tradition, the *Last Judgment*. The Blessed rise toward Christ, while on his left the sinners stream away in the four rivers of fire. This is the only large fresco in the Chapel in which the painter radically altered his figure size. Christ the Judge is abnormally large, and the Damned are extremely small. For Giotto the human figure was the emblem of religious and moral values, and he subjected it to diminution, indignity, or violence only *in extremis*.

GIOTTO, *ca.* 1303, EXPULSION OF JOACHIM
FROM THE TEMPLE Detail

Padua, Arena Chapel

This sublime painting begins the story of the life of the Virgin in the uppermost order of the Chapel. It is probably also, I believe, the first scene Giotto executed in the Chapel, painting at least the figures himself, without any assistance. Only the upper zone of the triumphal arch and the immediately succeeding scenes (pages 44, 47) show an equally brilliant and luscious brushwork, which does not exclude precision and even minuteness. Marvelous is the drama realized in the face of Joachim by the interplay of the green earth underpainting and the white and hot red laid over it.

The priest refuses Joachim's offering of a lamb and turns him out of the temple because he had given Israel no children. Unlike most earlier representations of this event the priest has no attendants, and there are no witnesses. The two confront each other alone—the stern, perhaps angry but certainly not unsympathetic priest, who exhibits a fundamental humanity during the performance of his official duty, and the anguished old man, still clinging tightly to his rejected lamb as though it were the child that God had denied him. Giotto has suggested very discreetly the consequences of this fateful meeting. At the left, more than half hidden behind a wall, a second priest blesses a young father. At the right, where Joachim must go, there is only a large void, an altogether unprecedented and highly expressive form. The old man, still retained within the solid structure of the temple, stands on the verge of an abyss.

The fresco is well preserved. Only the blue, added *a secco*, has adhered imperfectly, both in the background and in the tunic of Joachim. Where it has peeled from his sleeve and from the bottom of his skirt we are recompensed by a glimpse of the bold red and ocher strokes of Giotto's preparatory painting. The reproduction makes visible also the long, deep red lines the painter added for strong accents around the hand of the priest and Joachim's sleeve. We can see clearly, too, the brown strokes on the wall below the pulpit, constituting a large, and very early, cast shadow.

The lower part of the face and head of the young man who is blessed by a priest does not match the color of the upper part because it was painted afterward, on another patch of *intonaco*. When Giotto painted the upper part he intended only that much of the face to be visible above the wall. He then decided to add a mouth and a jaw, presumably to heighten the contrast of this quiet, receptive man with the rejected Joachim. To do this he had to lower the height of the enclosing wall.

GIOTTO, *ca.* 1303, JOACHIM RETURNS TO HIS SHEEPFOLD

Padua, Arena Chapel

Expelled from the temple, Joachim felt too much shame to return home and instead he went to his sheepfold. The bowed old man has just moved slowly and heavily into the space, while the shepherds and their flock have advanced to meet him. He is however alone in his profound dejection. Even his hands are wrapped in his isolating mantle. His dog, about to greet him joyfully, seems to arrest his leap as he senses trouble. The shepherds exchange glances about his despair and hold back discreetly. Though separated from Joachim by their postures and the wide interval of space they are nevertheless united in a common experience. They are all enfolded by a remarkably sensitive rock, and their thoughts are, as it were, joined by the lighted plane that flows quietly behind their heads. This is a drama of the mind.

The figures are almost like Gothic cathedral statues, uniform with the wall—here natural—of rock. The shallow but vivid space is measured inward left and right, and at the same time fenced, by Joachim and the shed. They are turned at corresponding angles. Between them the shepherds create a chiastic pattern, the one nearer Joachim placed at the angle of the shed, the one nearer the shed at the angle of Joachim. This firm but rhythmical order of verticals—the woof we might say—is interwoven with freer horizontal strands, all beginning or ending in the head of Joachim. One of these strands unites, as we have mentioned, the three heads and continues into the towering crag at the far right, which leads to the next scene. Another flows upward from the old man's halo along the crowns of the trees, and a third courses downward from him through the dog and sheep, or vice versa.

The scene, executed mostly in true fresco, is well preserved. Joachim would have been somewhat more accented originally when the blue of his tunic was visible on his breast and his skirt. As in the preceding scene only traces of this color, applied in tempera, remain.

46

GIOTTO AND ASSISTANTS, *ca.* 1304,

CHRIST DRIVING THE MERCHANTS FROM THE TEMPLE

Padua, Arena Chapel

In Giotto's superb cycle this is neither one of the most memorable frescoes nor the best preserved. It contains passages, however, of unsurpassed beauty, and the loss of blue applied in tempera gives us a unique insight into Giotto's mural practices early in his career.

When seen alone, the composition appears unbalanced. The temple is turned toward the right, and the movement of the figures, strong but cadenced and amplified by the arches, is opposed only by the conspiring priests at the extreme right. When designing this painting Giotto counted on the buttressing effect of the triumphal arch, which projects from this wall just beyond the fresco.

According to St. Matthew, Jesus entered the temple, cast out the merchants, and overthrew the tables of the money changers and the seats of the sellers of doves. When the priests saw what he did and saw the children that were crying and saying, Hosanna to the son of David, they were moved with indignation.

The Cleansing of the Temple was not often represented in monumental cycles, and Giotto's version contains fascinating and enigmatic innovations. First of all, as contaminators of the temple there are only the vendors of sacrificial birds and animals; the painter has practically eliminated the usual signs of the money changers—the falling scales, the careening table spilling coins, and the purses carried away by anxious owners. Of all this there remains at most a table lying face down, if indeed it is not the seat of "them that sell doves" mentioned by Matthew. Now the patron of the Chapel and the frescoes, Enrico Scrovegni, was the son of a notorious moneylender. The choice of the unusual scene, and then the suppression in it of references to money, indicate a remarkable ambivalence between an intention to confess or to expiate and a desire to conceal.

The children described in the Gospels had not appeared in earlier representations. Though in the text they hail Christ's angry triumph, in the fresco they flee from it, one sheltered by St. Peter, the other by a young apostle marvelously painted in a luminous, gray-green mantle. His covered face, in deep red shade, expresses withdrawal—a very human response at this moment, but astonishing even for Giotto and still to be fully explained.

The child holding the dove was an afterthought, added by cutting out and replacing the *intonaco* of part of Peter's mantle. The loss of the blue in Christ's mantle has disclosed the painter's quick sketch for the crate behind him. It does not quite correspond with the form painted. A curved red line that has "burned" through the paint reveals that Christ's face was at one moment placed a little further to the right and perhaps given a still more aggressive thrust. These and other changes prove that for Giotto no less than for later artists creation was a process of sustained searching. He was even willing to knock out plaster after the scene was finished.

48

GIOTTO, THE DEFEAT OF THE SULTAN'S PRIESTS

Florence, Santa Croce, Bardi Chapel

When St. Francis visited the Sultan in Egypt and tried to convert him to Christianity he proposed to prove the superiority of his God and his faith by walking into a fire. According to Bonaventura, who in his life of the Saint described the event, a priest of the Sultan who was standing nearby heard Francis speak and immediately fled. In the detail reproduced from the left half of the fresco, Giotto has depicted the consternation of the priest, who turns away and raises his mantle in a gesture of defense. A companion at the left reacts similarly, whereas a Moor points toward Francis and another close to the Sultan's throne watches.

Though the figures respond suddenly to the proposal of the Saint their actions compose a rhythmical design that absorbs even the abrupt excitement of the raised yellow mantle. The waves of opposed movement end in a balanced and harmonious composition. The figures are more imposing than those in the Arena Chapel, painted about two decades earlier; the drapery is wrapped more loosely, and the space is deeper.

The few surviving Giottesque murals of this period are either irreparably damaged or executed by assistants. This fresco seems to me one of the very few painted by the master himself. Such an assertion could not confidently have been made until 1958, when the original surface of all the frescoes in this chapel was skilfully freed of the alterations and the "unifying" film of tempera applied in a misguided restoration of 1853.

The yellow and white mantles and the white turbans have a Venetian luminosity and richness of texture. The brown flesh of the Moors, shaded in purple, is painted with equal brilliance. The mantles of the two figures at both extremities of the reproduction have lost their final color, which was applied *a secco*, and they therefore give us an opportunity to see Giotto's dashing preliminary painting. The folds of the drapery are so fully and decisively defined that we, familiar with the open brushwork and the sketchy definition of later centuries, might not read these areas as unfinished. Giotto could paint in two different modes, and though nowadays the sketchy one is preferred by many, the painter did not of course share this judgment for finished surfaces.

WORKSHOP OF GIOTTO, HEAD OF A SHEPHERD

Florence, Badia, Choir

★

This is the only head that was recovered in 1958 on the original wall of the choir of the Badia, behind a new wall that was built in the seventeenth century. It is a fragment from a scene of Joachim returning to his sheepfold, the same scene that Giotto himself painted in the Arena Chapel and that is reproduced on page 47.

Writing in the mid-fifteenth century the sculptor Lorenzo Ghiberti, a great admirer of early fourteenth-century painting and especially of Giotto, included the frescoes in the choir of the Badia in his list of Giotto's works. When the existence of some fragments of the cycle was established in 1940 historians hoped for new evidence that would resolve the difficult and much-debated questions of Giotto's early work. The recovery of the paintings, however, only added a new problem; they proved to be rather different in style from previously known works. Although some scholars date the Badia fragments in the twenties or thirties, they were probably executed in the early years of the century.

It is generally agreed that an assistant of Giotto painted the surviving frescoes. Though the shepherd has the same intent glance as the shepherds in the corresponding scene in the Arena Chapel, his head is not so solid and sculptural. The geometry and the luminous planes of the figure remain impressive, however, despite the damage, and altogether this fragment has an undeniable poetry.

TADDEO GADDI, ANNUNCIATION TO THE SHEPHERDS

Florence, Santa Croce, Baroncelli Chapel

Taddeo Gaddi, Cennini tells us in his manual, worked with Giotto for twenty-four years, and in this fresco Taddeo demonstrated his deep understanding of the coloristic principles of the great master's late work, as they were set forth in the fresco of the Sultan in the nearby Bardi Chapel (page 51). Indeed Taddeo applied Giotto's nuances of color and light to a display of supernatural illumination that is not approached by the surviving paintings of Giotto or any other earlier master.

According to St. Luke, shepherds in the country near Bethlehem were keeping watch by night over their flock when an angel appeared "and the glory of the Lord shone round about them." Taddeo depicted this glory in a new way. The principle of his innovation seems simple, at least after the fact. He darkened the usual hillside in this scene, the trees, and also the sky above, employing an unusual deep brown preparation. He carried his color down to a rich chocolate, borne by two animals. In this dusky environment the yellow light of the angel becomes incandescent. With great mastery Taddeo follows it as it touches the shepherds, the trees, and the beasts. Its warmth and subtle flow communicate beautifully the nature of the angel's tidings.

The two shepherds are at once closely identified in mass and shape yet decisively differentiated. The more distant one, his face entirely invisible, seems just aroused by the apparition and shields his eyes from the glare. His companion has already understood the message and hails the messenger. Most of the animals are still asleep, in charmingly varied positions, but below the shepherds two of them awaken, and the watchdog stares malevolently at the intruder.

The full beauty of this fresco became visible only nine years ago, when all the paintings in the chapel were cleaned. Apart from the loss of a patch of *intonaco* and of some blue in the sky it is remarkably well preserved. In the reproduction one can even see quite clearly the line of juncture between two patches of *intonaco* as it passes just above the animals. Another curving joint is visible in the dark preparatory color of the sky.

TADDEO GADDI AND WORKSHOP, TRANSFIGURATION

Florence, Badia

★

The fresco was discovered during the course of repair of the Badia a year after the flood of 1966. The niche in which it was painted had been, strangely enough, bricked up after 1924. Inasmuch as the fresco was deteriorating from dampness that still remained in the wall, restorers detached it and uncovered the stark, imposing *sinopia* under it.

The *sinopia* closely resembles the one under Taddeo's famous *Last Supper* in S. Croce, which was disclosed at the same time and for the same reason. They both record only the outlines of the figures, without any shading. Nevertheless these few lines define Christ, Moses, and Elijah so extensively that we can recognize the many alterations introduced in the fresco. The master may have asked an assistant to carry out the painting, for the figures are somewhat softer than his. Taddeo, indeed, normally seems to have painted with a copy of Berenson on "tactile values" in his left hand.

In this scene of the Transfiguration, it is true, the painter sought luminary more than plastic effects. He returned again to the depiction of supernatural radiance, which he had accomplished so brilliantly in the *Annunciation to the Shepherds* and which fascinated him throughout his career. Here again the yellow light blazes before a sky prepared in purple, much of which, through losses, has again become visible.

The apostles below who witness this event are so badly damaged that they are only partly included in the reproduction. One of them shields his eyes very much like an apostle in Fra Angelico's *Transfiguration* reproduced on page 116.

TADDEO GADDI, MADONNA DEL PARTO

Florence, San Francesco di Paola

★

Paintings such as this *Madonna* were frequently neglected when the admiration of fourteenth- and fifteenth-century painting waned in subsequent centuries. The lower part of this approximately life-size, standing figure was carelessly lost. The rest became so caked with dirt that only the head was visible. Removal from the wall and cleaning in 1964 restored to us yet another impressive painting by Taddeo Gaddi. The areas painted in fresco turned out to be well preserved, whereas only traces of the blue of the Madonna's mantle, executed *a secco*, remain. The surface under the blue in this cult image is very light, and hence quite unlike the preparation in the luminary miracles by Taddeo on pages 54, 57. Even the areas of shade were indicated only by patches of pale violet.

In medieval poetry and theology the Virgin was often described as the vase or the tabernacle of Christ, and the idea of Christ in her womb had occasionally been given symbolic form in art. The image of a simple gravid mother, however, was introduced only in the second quarter of the fourteenth century in Florence, and Taddeo's fresco is one of the first examples. The Madonna del Parto appeared at the same time and in the same region—Tuscany—as other new subjects such as the Madonna of Humility or the Holy Family that similarly presented Mary and related figures in novel human and even domestic guise.

Taddeo's Virgin, like some other early images of this type, wears a high girdle, holds a book in one hand and refers discreetly to her condition with the other. The book symbolizes the Bible or, more generally, Christian doctrine and learning. Only a few representations of the pregnant Mary are known, most of them Italian of the fourteenth and fifteenth centuries, and we therefore identify the image by its Italian title, *Madonna del Parto*.

MASTER OF THE FOGG PIETÀ, *ca.* 1345, HEAD OF ST. ONOPHRIUS

Florence, Sant' Ambrogio

★

The plate shows the head of an approximately life-size representation of the Early Christian hermit Onophrius. The figure came to light as a great surprise in 1965 underneath a fresco datable only about thirty years later and representing a different subject. The technique is unusual because the figure was drawn on the damp *intonaco* in two shades of red and gray, and then perhaps tinted *a secco*, though none of this pigment remains. This rare example of a monumental colored drawing served, furthermore, as a completed image over an altar.

The author of the work, one of Giotto's greatest successors, gave the Saint an imposing physical presence. With a searching line he at once defined forms, such as eyebrows or cheekbone, and endowed them with an intense emotional life. The head, surrounded by great masses of heaving hair, is unsurpassed for powerful feeling in fourteenth-century Florence.

MASO DI BANCO, MIRACLES OF ST. SYLVESTER *(overleaf)*

Florence, Santa Croce

Emperor Constantine, who had been baptized by Sylvester, asked him to control a dragon that lived in a cave in the Roman Forum and was slaying three hundred men a day with its foul breath alone. In the fresco Sylvester, dressed as pope and accompanied by two deacons, binds the jaws of the monster in the cave and brings back to life two of its victims. The Emperor watches with approval.

In medieval representations of Sylvester's miracles a couple of columns identified the Forum. Inspired by the site, which he may have visited, Maso went beyond symbolism to describe the irregular and accidental disintegration of buildings during the passage of time. Stones from the large broken arch litter the ground. Maso seems to allude to ancient Roman architectural style, and he clearly indicated that the decay occurred in the past, because plants have taken root in the broken walls. There had been no such depiction in all of post-classical art. Maso evoked the sentiment of a lost past, and he introduced here the modern conception of a historical ruin.

(continued on page 62)

The painter was referring, no doubt, to the decline of pagan Rome. Nevertheless his buildings, which have an unprecedented depth and scale, enhance the majesty of the Christian miracle, with which they are always intimately connected. At the center the Saint is enframed by two white walls and crowned by a red arch. His spiritual power descends to the two risen men along

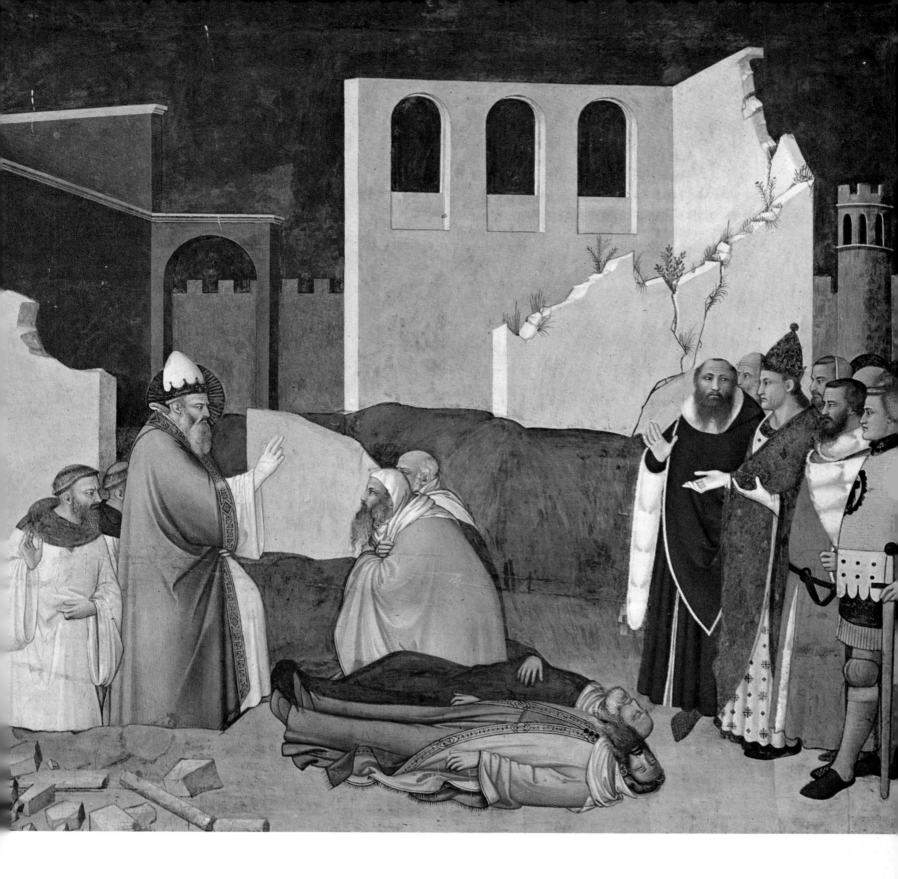

the curving wall that passes to their heads. The large broken arch repeats many curves throughout the composition; it appears above the now "broken" dragon, which composes a similar but opposed arc. These superb interrelationships of shape are enriched by a no less subtle and beautiful pattern of color, somewhat hardened by retouching forty years ago.

LUCA DELLA ROBBIA, 1454–1459, TOMB OF BISHOP FEDERIGHI

Florence, Santa Trinita

ATTRIBUTED TO ALESSO DI ANDREA, *ca.* 1343, PAINTED TOMB

Prato, Cathedral, Crypt

The frescoed tomb, reproduced at the right, rather inaccessible and scarcely known to historians until 1963, was painted in the writer's opinion by a pupil of Maso whose name was discovered in 1964. Among surviving tombs simulated in fresco the painting in Prato creates the most complete illusion because the figures are practically life-size and the structure fills an entire wall; the lowest part, which extends to the floor, has been severely damaged and is therefore not reproduced. The effigy of the unidentified deceased simulates white stone, the architecture veined marble. The Man of Sorrows, the Virgin and St. John, however, appear in full color against a background of blue (mostly lost) over red. How are we to understand them, as painted reliefs or as supernatural apparitions at the rear openings of the tomb? These figures, associated with Intercession and Redemption, had often appeared earlier in sculptured tombs, but below the effigy, in relief on the sarcophagus.

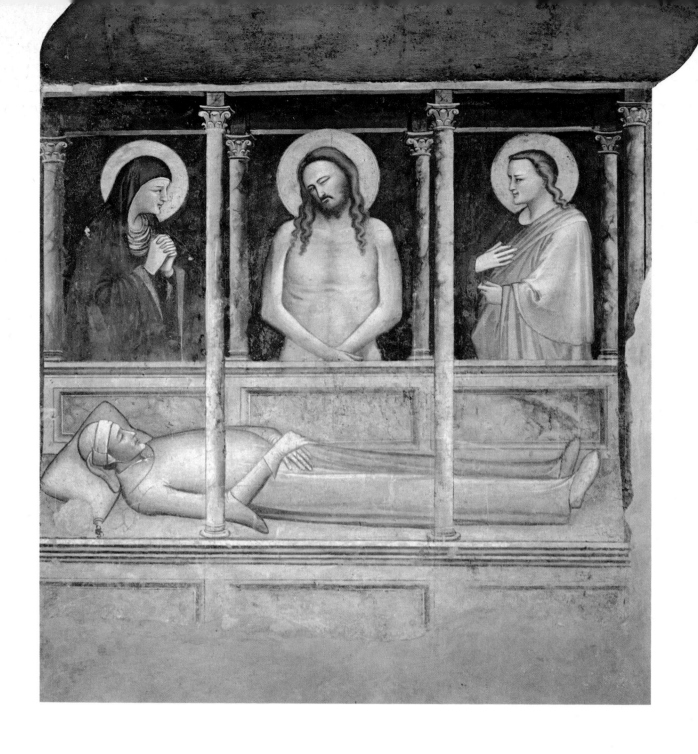

With respect to its rectangular structure and the place of the sacred figures within it Alesso's composition is unique among all fourteenth-century tombs, whether simulated or actual. The first surviving tomb that resembles it, and that may reflect it, is the monument made a century later by Luca della Robbia. The sculptures are surrounded by a beautiful border in the pictorial technique of glazed terracotta. The differences between painting and sculpture were, as so often, further reduced by the gilding (now largely lost) of the halos, the angels' wings, and the mitre, stole and cushion of the bishop.

ALESSO DI ANDREA, 1347, HOPE

Pistoia, Cathedral

Hope is one of a group of four Virtues painted on the jambs of a window in 1347 in what was then a chapel. The window was walled up in 1379, and the paintings remained protected from light, air and moisture until their discovery in 1953. As frescoes that were exposed only thirty years the *Virtues* are unique, and their state of preservation is unusually good, despite some small losses and stains. We still have the last touches of the painter's brush, the highlights on the ear and chin or the black bands of shadow in the folds of the mantle. Even the surface painted in tempera, the beautifully graduated rose of the halo, survives intact. Virtues, it should be said, commonly wear hexagonal halos; the circular form was reserved for saints.

For *Hope*, as for the other Virtues, the painter transformed the wall into an architectural canopy about 2^1/$_2$ feet deep that opens onto the limitless space of the refulgent gold. When constructing the perspective of the canopy he took account of the place of the fresco; it is above the head of the observer and on the left jamb of the window, and he chose for this Virtue and the one above it a point of view toward the left, in the chapel.

The design embodies a principle of illusionism that was developed by the ancient Romans, as we have seen, and that survived in Italian medieval painting in such forms as the brackets in the *Creation of Eve* (page 36). It was the fresco painters of the first half of the fourteenth century who learned how to design such vivid fictive structures as the tabernacle of *Hope*. The figure utilizes the constructed space by turning inward toward the floating crown, but the painter has lighted the head so brightly that he has given it prominence at some sacrifice of spatial consistency. It is true, however, that the corner of the halo that now may seem to overlap the arch in front of it was originally covered by the black band of the cusp.

The discovery of these frescoes has also restored to us the painter Alesso, for documents indicate that they are very probably his work. Though we possess very few facts about him, the style of the *Virtues* shows that he was a pupil of Maso di Banco. That master's refinement of color guided Alesso's subtle variation of red in the fresco of *Hope*, ranging from the carnation of the flesh and the glowing rose halo to the violet spandrel with its deep maroon inlay.

PIETRO LORENZETTI, *ca.* 1315, MADONNA

Assisi, San Francesco, Lower Church, Orsini Chapel

About 1305, as the great campaign to paint the walls and vaults of the Upper Church neared completion, the Franciscans turned to the older Lower Church. They decided to fresco, or to fresco again in a newer style, the transepts and the crossing, and to begin the decoration of the new chapels that were being added to the church. For this work the friars brought to Assisi, beginning about 1306, followers of Giotto and, for the first time, Sienese painters, who were just becoming skilled in the art of fresco. Both Pietro Lorenzetti and Simone Martini, whose paintings in the Lower Church appear on the accompanying plate and the following three, worked there as young masters.

When the Franciscans engaged painters to participate in the large enterprise they kept in mind the effect of the whole. Instead of commissioning the usual panels for the two prominent altars at the opposite ends of the transept, which face each other, they chose large triptychs for positions about ten feet over each of the altars. These triptychs, executed in fresco, maintained a uniformity with the frescoes on the walls. The Madonna and saints in both, furthermore, are framed by fictive architecture that is related to the real structure of the church. These paintings are among the earliest, and certainly the best altarpieces simulated in the new technique of fresco.

Until about 1900 the frescoed frame above Pietro's *Madonna* was preserved intact. When a strip of the plaster fell out the loss was replaced by a substance that is now black. Although only traces of the red pigment painted *a secco* on the mantle of the Child remain, and part of the gold background has been lost, the rest of the *Madonna* is in good condition. The subtle chiaroscuro of her face is superb.

In this fresco, one of Pietro's earliest works, he still speaks to us with the eloquence of his teacher Duccio. The tenderness of the angels, the sinuous golden lines of the Madonna's mantle, and the soft rich texture of her white scarf all recall the older master. Pietro has however transformed the more generalized sentiment of Duccio's Madonnas into a grave, sad brooding. The Child, who grasps her scarf and her finger, seems to seek her attention in vain. She is well aware of him, however, for she holds him close to her with a firm, powerful hand.

WORKSHOP OF PIETRO LORENZETTI, LAST SUPPER Detail

Assisi, San Francesco, Lower Church

Not long after painting the triptych of the Madonna and Saints Pietro Lorenzetti moved out of the chapel into the south transept to begin scenes of the Passion of Christ. He was joined by assistants, one of whom resembles the so-called Dijon Master. The fresco cycle is full of surprises, above all this view of the kitchen in which the Passover dinner was prepared for what became the Last Supper. The cleaning of heavy deposits of carbon five years ago from the scenes as well as from the borders containing prophets in quatrefoils has disclosed a beautiful subtlety of color.

For the first time a painter envisaged with considerable consistency a space illuminated by a light within it. The wood fire in the chimney brightens almost everything in the kitchen, leaving in shade principally the two bins on the far wall, though even here its rosy hue warms a corner of each horizontal plane. Most extraordinary of all, the cat and the dog, very close to the source of all this light, throw shadows on the floor. The shadows were not painted onto the fresco surface but are contained within it, so they are beyond doubt original. Since these frescoes are in my opinion no later than the twenties and probably earlier, these shadows, not hitherto described, are the first of their kind we know. Indeed, shadows cast onto the ground can be found again only a century later.

It is interesting that these shadows appear close to a brilliant light and are associated with animals. No sacred figure in any of the scenes casts shadows. At this time such shadows belong, as the reproduction shows, to a "slice of life" that is governed by a different mode of seeing. The entire kitchen is unprecedented alongside a Last Supper, and even the presence in the dining room of two men engaged in conversation—the richly dressed figure is probably the host mentioned in the Gospels—is rare. All of this occurs at the moment when Christ identifies his betrayer, the hook-nosed Judas, by handing him a "sop," and historians often describe the secondary incidents as ignoble profanation. They are, however, really only bold and rather extreme manifestations of a widespread intention, especially among the Franciscans, to bring the traditional stories close to the life of the fourteenth century. We encounter this purpose in the religious poetry of the time, which dwells on practical, domestic aspects of the existence of the Holy Family, describing their means of earning a livelihood and the endeavors of the youthful Jesus to help. In the frescoes of Pietro's brother, Ambrogio, we shall find other, striking consequences of this wish to give a more familiar setting and a deeper humanity to the traditional Christian subjects.

SIMONE MARTINI, ST. MARTIN BEFORE EMPEROR JULIAN

Assisi, San Francesco, Lower Church, Chapel of St. Martin

Simone Martini, the second great Sienese painter called to Assisi, arrived there soon after Pietro Lorenzetti to paint one of the chapels added to the nave of the Lower Church. The subject of the cycle was the legend of St. Martin, the patron of the founder of the chapel, the Cardinal of San Martino ai Monti.

The *Golden Legend* served as the painter's principal source. The scene reproduced shows the young Saint, a member of the Roman imperial guard, addressing Emperor Julian. Julian, encamped at Worms, had decided to make a gift to his men, and just behind him a bursar drops gold coins into the open palm of a helmeted soldier. Martin, who did not wish to bear arms any longer, refused the gift, saying that he was a knight of Christ. Accused of fear by the Emperor, Martin replied that on the morrow he would go unarmed into the lines of the enemy, bearing only the cross. It is this dramatic moment that Simone represents. The barbarians, formidably armed and warring under the sign of an aggressive rampant lion, appear nearby behind a hill on a river that may represent the Rhine. The next day, before Martin's arrival, the barbarians miraculously laid down their weapons.

Simone was a painter who knew how to give the Emperor and his entourage an appropriate pomp, though it has been diminished by the disappearance or oxidation of much of the metallic pigment on the armor and the faldstool. Even the imperial double-eagles, on the golden shields of the tents, have peeled off.

Simone recreates the story as a sort of tense, colorful dance. The rhythmical payment of the gold coins before a blue tent-pole, the astonished, indignant Emperor pointing his scepter at Martin, the stolid bodyguards wearing the same color as the mountains, all this culminates in the Saint who, to clarify his intention, rotates toward the barbarians. The turn is continued by the mountain and the river. High against the sky a peak points in the same general direction.

The fresco contains innumerable subtleties, but even if many more were described the result would still be not much more than a diagram. Fortunately the reader has a good reproduction of Simone's work in full color.

SIMONE MARTINI, MUSICIANS

Detail of Knighting of St. Martin

Assisi, San Francesco, Lower Church, Chapel of St. Martin

Whereas the preceding plate shows St. Martin leaving the Roman army this one, representing a prior episode, shows him joining it. Martin's father was a tribune or knight, the *Golden Legend* says. Following an imperial decree that the sons of veterans should fight with their fathers, Martin, then fifteen years old, received the spurs and sword from the Emperor.

The investiture of Martin as a knight was occasionally represented earlier, but the celebration of the event by a company of musicians seems to have been conceived by Simone Martini. It is one of those transformations of a traditional subject that are so characteristic of Central Italian painting of this time. Simone, the creator of the most exquisite art of the century, was a perfect choice for the depiction of elegant ceremonies at court. His imagination drifted in general less to kitchens or extreme states of mind than to subtle feelings and the mysterious moods of music. Three times in his surviving early works he painted men rapt in song. Here he added players of a double recorder and a mandola. They wear the gay, divided dress of the time. The beautiful though worn and somewhat altered green now looks like moss.

The men are moved by the sounds of their music. The mandola player, entirely absorbed, looks into the distance. His companion with the recorders glances past us with fleeting, enigmatic sentiments. His intriguing face seems a true precursor of Leonardo's mysterious countenances. Vasari tells us, indeed, that Leonardo produced the expression he wanted for the *Mona Lisa* by persuading the sitter to listen to music.

PIETRO LORENZETTI, ST. JOHN

Detail of the Crucifixion

Siena, San Francesco

Until quite recently most persons, including many historians of art, did not understand what they were seeing when they looked at Italian mural paintings. As a young scholar the writer himself was puzzled by this *Crucifixion* and similar works, and the questions he put to his older colleagues did not diminish his ignorance. The reader, however, will probably already have recognized that most of the surface in this detail was not intended to be seen once the work was finished. Only the flesh and hair of the figure were completed in fresco and they remain almost intact. The final colors of the background (blue) and of the mantle and tunic (perhaps rose and blue) were executed *a secco* and have disappeared, leaving only the preliminary painting done in true fresco.

Only preliminary painting! But how powerful an image of despair it defines! To relieve, and at the same time control, his deep feeling St. John grips his hands tightly, creating a strain felt throughout his two strong arms. He twists his head down over his shoulder, and the massive folds of the mantle, which continue the movement, seem further to depress his body.

Pietro originally painted his *Crucifixion* in the chapter room of the seminary, and when the painting together with its plaster support was transferred more than a century ago to a chapel in the church, the lower part was broken off, so that the figure of St. John is incomplete. All the surviving surface that we see, executed in true fresco, was apparently painted, with the speed normal at that time, in less than a day.

In the mantle and tunic the bare *intonaco* serves for the nearer, lighted areas. Pietro's brush streaks across the surface to create shade and define volume, sweeping into shallow valleys and gouging out the dark hollows. His strokes usually follow the curvature of the planes. All of this was replaced in the final painting by more graduated transitions from light to dark, and by the absorption of the strokes of the brush into the areas of color.

The signs of the process of creation that we, centuries later, find moving, Pietro and his contemporaries judged not suitable for finished work. In the sixteenth century Vasari described the art of Pietro's period as "dry," but we may infer that Pietro in turn would have found the painting of Vasari and his era loose and unfinished. Time and death are irreversible; we have the judgments of later artists about their predecessors, but not the opposite. These circumstances, unless corrected by knowledge, can deceive us and promote a biased view of artists and of artistic history.

AMBROGIO LORENZETTI AND WORKSHOP, 1338–1339,

THE GOOD CITY   Detail

Siena, Palazzo Pubblico, Council Chamber

In the independent Italian cities fresco had become an art for the masses, a medium for propaganda but without the commercialization that poisons comparable arts in our time. In 1315 the elected rulers of the republic of Siena had engaged Simone Martini to cover a wall of the great council room of the town hall with a fresco of the Madonna and a host of saints. As the patroness and divine ruler of the city she speaks to its councilors in words inscribed below the fresco, enjoining them to act justly, unselfishly, and in the public interest. A generation later Ambrogio Lorenzetti was commissioned to communicate similar ideas in the adjoining council chamber, which was likewise a public room. On one wall Ambrogio painted an allegory of justice and the common good, and on a second wall an allegory of tyranny.

The third wall, over forty feet long, shows the city of Siena and the countryside enjoying good government. The inscription below this fresco, the largest and most important of its kind that we know, contains phrases such as "You who rule turn your eyes to admire Justice who is depicted here and gives each his due. Behold how much good comes from her and how sweet life is and how tranquil." On the scroll of *Securitas* who flies above is written "Without fear everyone goes about freely."

The detail reproduced is a small section of the city near the wall. A heavily laden donkey comes into town through the main gate—Siena is a city of rose brick. Just ahead another donkey moves up a narrow street, and a third, bearing wood, is driven into a street that begins behind a shop. There are two open shops, traditional in Italy since Roman times. One of them displays sausages, cured meat, and jugs of various liquids; in the other three artisans work on cloth. Copper or brass pots hang outside a shop in the side street. The painter has caught beautifully the posture and gait of the young woman carrying on her head a large basket of wash. An older woman wearing a pearly green skirt follows with a fowl in her arms.

Ambrogio, the outstanding master of perspective in the fourteenth century, effectively represents the city rising from the region reproduced. Light strikes in from the left, illuminating some flowers in a pot on a window sill, and leaving in shadow the curve of each of the arches. Though the paint is unevenly preserved the fresco still gives us the most vivid portrayal of a medieval town that has come down to us—its narrow streets filled with animals as well as people, its shared life, even, by modern standards, its coziness.

AMBROGIO LORENZETTI AND ASSISTANT, ANNUNCIATION

Fresco altered by Assistant of Pietro Lorenzetti

Montesiepi, Oratory of San Galgano

★

St. Luke says that at the time of the Annunciation the first words Gabriel spoke to Mary troubled her, and quite early Sienese painters depicted this initial, very human response of the Virgin to the angel by a kind of defensive withdrawal. Sometimes, too, in the second quarter of the fourteenth century—the period of our composition—they represented her humility at this moment by seating her upon the floor. No artist, however, before the author of the *sinopia*, and perhaps none later, portrayed the Virgin so overcome by the apparition that she shrinks to the floor and hugs a column for support. Her diverse movements are realized by a cluster of bold, sure strokes. Gabriel is evoked by even fewer lines.

Shortly after the completion of the fresco the unorthodox figure was transformed into a more conventional Virgin who, standing and facing the angel, humbly accepts the

message by bowing toward him while crossing her hands on her breast. To effect this change another painter, very close (it seems to the writer) to Pietro Lorenzetti, Ambrogio's brother, took over. He cut out a patch of the original *intonaco* above the crouching Virgin, replaced it, and then painted the new head and hands in true fresco, according to normal practice. He repainted much of the original figure in a *secco* technique and the paint has as usual flaked off, disclosing once again the original Virgin Mary, especially the telling head and eyes, which were executed in true fresco. Somewhat later the tonsured man kneeling in prayer behind the angel, now rather faint, was likewise added in *secco* to the original composition.

The transformation of the Virgin soon after the completion of the fresco can scarcely reflect dissatisfaction of the original artist with his innovation, for it was another master who replaced it. We know very few alterations of this kind, so that the existence of a similar one in the fresco of the Majesty of the Virgin (reproduced here) immediately above the *Annunciation* is all the more fascinating. Here the first master painted an equally novel Mary, for she was represented as a crowned empress holding a scepter and an orb. Eve lies at her feet, and the entire image was probably inspired by St. Bernard's vision of the exalted Virgin in canto XXXII of Dante's *Paradise*. St. Bernard was the greatest saint of the Cistercian order, to which the oratory of Montesiepi belonged. The two frescoes expressed related ideas, especially with regard to Christ's redemption of Eve's sin by assuming, at the time of the Annunciation, a human form. The second painter eliminated the imperial attributes of the Virgin and showed her holding her child. What the changes in the two frescoes have in common, then, is the substitution of a conventional image for a highly unconventional one. In the *Majesty* the Virgin was rendered less exalted and more maternal, in the *Annunciation* she became less emotional and more pious. In the latter she certainly became also less problematic — for her first viewers as well as for us.

We may know the sources for some unusual aspects of the *Annunciation*. The palm held by the angel and the spread wings were probably suggested by the same passage in Dante that influenced the representation of the Virgin as empress; and the column as a support may perhaps be traced to a legend of the Annunciation current in the Holy Land, though the setting, a grotto, does not conform to the fresco. But a terrified Virgin Mary dropping to the floor is not described in any source yet cited.

Is the Virgin Mary a young woman overwhelmed by sudden awareness of the Incarnation?

Does her extreme behavior indicate that she also has a sudden foreknowledge of the Passion? Both these possibilities conform with known tendencies of the art of Ambrogio Lorenzetti. He was a learned painter who frequently introduced unusual subjects or attributes and deepened the reference of religious paintings. At the same time he, more than any other artist, transformed the Christ Child into a lively baby, and he could carry the humaniziation of the Virgin so far that, in his *Crucifixion* in the Fogg Museum, she lies unconscious on the ground below the cross. When describing another, lost, *Annunciation* by Ambrogio, a sixteenth-century writer singled out the agitation of the Virgin.

For these and other reasons it is difficult to dissociate the Montesiepi compositions from Ambrogio Lorenzetti, but equally difficult to be certain of his own hand, even in the extraordinary *sinopia*. Though we possess no *sinopia* by him for comparison, drawings on the *intonaco* of a few frescoes painted by him have become visible where the paint has flaked off and they do not quite confirm the attribution. At least the model of the figures, however, must have been by Ambrogio himself.

AMBROGIO LORENZETTI AND ASSISTANT,

MADONNA AND SAINTS Detail

Siena, Sant' Agostino

The plate opposite reproduces the central and best part of a fresco of the Madonna with saints and angels that was sealed from view in 1596 by a large altarpiece and found behind it in 1943.

The discovery of this fresco extends our understanding of fourteenth-century painting no less than the discovery of the Montesiepi *sinopia*, and in precisely the same direction. The subject is equally surprising and rare. In Madonnas of the time a bird, usually a goldfinch, often appears, held by either the Virgin or the Child, who sometimes has it on a string. The bird may symbolize the soul, of which Christ is the shepherd, or a series of ideas such as the Passion (clearly when it pecks at grain, as in Francesco Traini), the Resurrection, Death and the plague. In the S. Agostino *Madonna* the bird acts in a most unusual way, opening its beak and flapping its wings. Still more unusual is the action of the wide-eyed Child, who is clearly startled and terrified. Does he foresee his future, symbolized by the bird? If he looks beyond the bird, as seems quite possible, he sees a gruesome sight. St. Bartholomew presses forward the knife that flayed him and St. Catherine her severed head. Just beyond, St. Agatha extends her breasts on a salver. These saints as well as the bird confront Christ with the idea and indeed with the consequences of martyrdom, and he responds to them essentially as a child.

The action of the Child in this fresco is thus exactly like that of the Virgin in the Montesiepi *sinopia* and the unconscious Virgin below the cross in Ambrogio's panel in the Fogg Museum. It is quite like the action of the Virgin in contemporary religious literature, who implores Christ not to go to Jerusalem and thus to refuse to accept his preordained mission. It is therefore not unlikely that a human approach to the Christian mysteries would be taken by a great, cultivated artist such as Ambrogio Lorenzetti. Ambrogio adopted it, indeed, in other paintings. There is, furthermore, another representation of the Christ Child repelled by a goldfinch, and the author of this later work—a round marble relief in Burlington House, London—is Michelangelo.

In the Lorenzettian fresco the Madonna and Child are enclosed by the great spread wings of the seraphim, whose fiery red seems to express perfectly the mood of the moment. Much of the blue on the Virgin's mantle has come off, exposing the handsome yellow-brown underpainting.

BARNA DA SIENA, CRUCIFIXION

San Gimignano, Collegiata

This fresco, about twenty feet high, is part of a large cycle of the Passion that extends the length of the church to the transept. Except for the loss of blue in the lower sky it was well preserved until the recent World War, when the area below the cross now painted a disturbing blue was destroyed by a shell. In the lunette above is visible part of the *Massacre of the Innocents*.

During the first half of the fourteenth century Sienese painters had gradually transformed the relatively emblematic medieval conception of the Crucifixion into the depiction of a moment in time, full of sudden actions and immediate emotional responses. Working within this Sienese tradition and using exceptionally deep and sombre colors Barna heightened the sorrow of some figures and the violence of others. The angels grieve wildly, the pale Virgin swoons to the ground, a soldier forces his lance into Christ's chest, and another draws far back to strike again the bloodied legs of the thief on the cross. The agonized writhing of this thief is unmatched in the art of the time. The centurion, pointing to Christ, proclaims his conversion to several peering companions. While representing exceptionally high-pitched and therefore transitory emotion, Barna has also given the scene a novel extension in space. Figures not only seem to exist at the sides behind the frames but for the first time they appear on a declining slope behind the cross. All this seething movement is contained in a clear, imposing rhythmical design.

FRANCESCO TRAINI, THE DAMNED

Details of the Last Judgment *(opposite and overleaf)*

Pisa, Camposanto

From the period of their rapid growth in the thirteenth century the Italian city-states competed bitterly with each other and were torn by internal strife. They were divided also by the struggle between the Papacy and the secular power of the Holy Roman Emperor. Occasionally these conflicts left their mark on paintings and sculpture. Representations of the Last Judgment offered special opportunities, for in them it was found possible to allude to allies among the Blessed and to enemies among the Damned. For such a practice the *Divine Comedy* of Dante, written during the first two decades of the fourteenth century, served as a great model; in it Hell is heavily populated with those whom the poet judged to be enemies of the Florentine state.

We may gain an insight into contemporary conflicts by examining more carefully than has hitherto been done the *sinopia* for the huge fresco of the Last Judgment in Pisa's cemetery. This *sinopia* was revealed by the detachment of the powerful fresco, which had been damaged and discolored (chiefly reddened) by fire during the war. The section of the *sinopia* reproduced overleaf shows the group of the Damned nearest the flames of Hell. Two of them are about to be pulled into the fire by large hooks wielded by devils. Prominent among these major sinners are a pope, identifiable by his tiara, a mitred bishop, and a cardinal. The cardinal, grasping one of his companions to resist the pull of the devils, looks desperately out toward the observer. The draughtsman has treated him exceptionally by modeling his large hat in light and shade.

In the corresponding section of the fresco every one of these high ecclesiastics has been eliminated. The only representatives of the Church are two simple friars. Since the Camposanto was a great public monument it was probably not the whim of the painter but current conflicts and institutional preferences that determined the kinds of persons to be put in Hell. Historians have only recently begun to speculate about what these might be.

Traini's Hell is the most terrifying spectacle in fourteenth-century painting. Through his exceptional mastery of the movement of the face and body he realized overwhelming studies in extreme emotion, each figure conveying in a different way a unique kind of anguish and despair.

ORCAGNA, *ca.* 1360, THE DAMNED IN HELL

Detail

Florence, Santa Croce, Museo dell'Opera

★

The awesome fate that the group in Traini's fresco faced (page 91) has now overwhelmed the men and women in the accompanying plate. They have passed through the portal into the swirling fire, their ears filled with Dante's terrible words that are inscribed on the fresco itself: "You who enter, abandon every hope." Two men, their limbs entwined with serpents, plunge swords into each other while a devil breathing fire tugs at one of them. A partially armed soldier brandishes his sword before a woman who apparently implores him not to employ it.

Orcagna's Damned are much larger than Giotto's in the Arena Chapel (page 43). The intensity of his art and the inexorable violence he depicts seem to correspond with the grim religious experience of the third quarter of the century, especially as it was expressed by the great Dominican preacher Passavanti, whose sermons in Florence Orcagna no doubt heard. Preaching in 1354, a few years before the painting of the fresco, Passavanti said: "One day a French nobleman wondered if the damned in hell would be freed after a thousand years, and his reason told him no; he wondered again if after a hundred thousand years, if after a million years, if after as many thousands of years as there are drops of water in the sea, and once again his reason told him no."

This is one of the very few surviving fragments of a huge *Last Judgment* that was rediscovered in 1942 behind a later altar and detached from the wall in 1958. One would expect the letters on the banner to refer to Dante's Prodigals, but the imagery does not correspond. A second fragment of the cycle to which the *Last Judgment* belongs is reproduced on the following plate.

ORCAGNA, *ca.* 1360, THE BLIND AND HALT APPEAL TO DEATH

Florence, Santa Croce, Museo dell'Opera

★

This fragment comes from the lower left corner of a huge fresco, about twenty feet high and sixty feet long, small parts of which were discovered in this century, detached, and then flooded in 1966. This part of the fresco, which represents the so-called Triumph of Death, was followed by a Last Judgment and Hell, one fragment of which is reproduced in the preceding plate. This gigantic admonition was painted ten or fifteen years after the troubles that overwhelmed Florence and Tuscany at the time, especially the Black Death of 1348. Traini painted a similar cycle on an equal scale in the Camposanto in Pisa; details of his *Last Judgment* are reproduced on pages 89, 91. In the opinion of the writer, but not of all historians, Traini's composition was the earlier.

The *Triumph of Death* in Pisa, which is preserved in its entirety, provides a composition into which we can fit Orcagna's fragments and thus interpret them. His crippled man and woman are gazing at a great flying figure of Death, which they watch with a marvelous catlike concentration. The two blind men above, one with an unseeing eye, the other with closed lids, sense the presence of the Reaper. They cry out: "Since prosperity has abandoned us, O Death, medicine of every pain, come give us now the last supper." Their desperate appeal falls on deaf ears. Death, an old woman wielding a scythe, continues to fly toward a "prosperous" group who will be struck down, in accordance with the inscription: "Neither learning, riches, high birth nor bravery count for anything against her blows."

Because this part of Orcagna's composition was painted in fresco and then skillfully detached and remounted it has survived well even immersion in the recent flood waters and in the fuel oil that they bore.

NARDO DI CIONE, *ca.* 1357, HEAD OF AN APOSTLE (SIMON?)

Florence, Santa Maria Novella, Strozzi Chapel

Nardo and his brother Orcagna worked together in the chapel of the Strozzi family in the great Dominican church in Florence. Orcagna completed the imposing altarpiece in 1357, and Nardo painted the frescoes about the same time. On the three high walls of the chapel Nardo painted frescoes similar in subject to those executed probably five to ten years later by Orcagna in Santa Croce, reproduced in the two preceding plates. Instead however of a Triumph of Death Nardo painted a *Gloria* or a *Paradise*, Christ and the Virgin enthroned amidst the heavenly host. In the uppermost of ten rows of saints that rise at both sides are the apostles. Though it is difficult to be certain, the attributes of the apostle reproduced point to St. Simon, who often bears the sword with which he was killed, and who frequently wears a yellow mantle. In the fresco the blade of the sword, which extends downward and was no doubt painted *a secco*, has disappeared. Behind and to the left of the apostle appear the folded hands of an angel, painted entirely in light blue. Some of the darker blue of the background has peeled off, disclosing a dark red preparatory color.

The fresco suffered so greatly from dampness through the centuries that it was partly repainted in the early eighteenth century. Since the deterioration continued, the enormous painting was detached from the wall two years ago, and the photograph was made in the conservator's studio after this part of the surface had been cleaned. Much of the yellow in the mantle has been lost, but the head is well preserved.

Though Nardo's images were milder than his brother's, we encounter here even in *Paradise* much of the incisiveness and tension that Orcagna gave to the crippled and the damned. The strands of hair curl out from the head with the stiffness of wire. The slashed lids, knit brows, and spare fingers heighten the sense of repressed emotion in this stern apostle.

GIOVANNI DA MILANO, 1365, MEETING OF JOACHIM AND ANNA

Florence, Santa Croce, Rinuccini Chapel

This episode in the story of the Virgin's parents follows shortly upon the expulsion of the childless Joachim from the temple and his return to his sheepfold, represented by Giotto in the Arena Chapel and reproduced on pages 44, 47. The angel, visible here in the upper left corner, is telling Joachim that Anna, though aged, has miraculously conceived, and instructs him to meet her at the Golden Gate of Jerusalem. There, the religious texts say, they greeted each other joyfully, and Anna "hung upon Joachim's neck."

The encounter in Giovanni's fresco departs from this description. Though Joachim and Anna grasp each other, they remain at arm's length. They do not even exchange glances; both seem wrapped in their own thoughts. Joachim's servant and Anna's companions maintain the solemnity of the meeting; they too are meditative and refrain from looking at the principal figures. The painter has transformed a happy family reunion into a formal encounter that stresses the miraculous nature of Anna's conception of Mary.

This change from familiar human response to action that approaches grave ritual is characteristic of Tuscan art of the third quarter of the fourteenth century. Characteristic of this art also is the rather abrupt alternation of warm and cool colors; the yellow mantle of Anna even has green shadows. Giovanni modeled his turning planes with extraordinary subtlety, producing surfaces almost as smooth and polished, and seemingly as hard, as glazed ceramics. The line is tight and incisive, especially in the oval around Joachim's shoulder and in the outlines of the women below the arch. The buildings, set at different angles and bristling with corbels and crenelations, add excitement and staccato accents to the scene.

Except for losses in the dog, in the ground around Joachim's servant, and in the red tunic at the right, the fresco is well preserved. For the hem of Anna's tunic and her shoe we now have only the preparatory painting.

Padua, Chapel of St. George

The chapel that contains this fresco is not far from the Arena Chapel (page 42), and the donor, Raimondino de' Lupi, animated by the same votive and mortuary purpose as Enrico Scrovegni, erected a building that is similar in scale and in shape. Here also one master with assistants painted the entire interior, and his art was developed through prolonged study of Giotto's. Though some frescoes suffered damage over the centuries, many of them were well preserved until recently, when air pollution and moisture began to take their toll. The reproduction shows one of the few areas that has been largely spared.

The *Crucifixion* is a large fresco on the wall above the altar. The figures, no less massive than Giotto's, are also distributed in clear, geometric patterns. In this detail the women compose an arc, which is then echoed by the forms above.

Though a Virgin Mary swooning below the Cross was occasionally described in medieval religious literature, the image was introduced in art only in the fourteenth century in Italy, as one of those many representations that presented a more natural human behavior of the sacred figures and thus elicited a new kind of emotional participation among the beholders. Mary's face is pallid, unrelieved by the rose blush that Altichiero normally places on cheeks. The painter has taken a radical step in the depiction of her anguish by abandoning the traditional deep blue of her mantle for a cold gray-blue—in fact, a gray-white color over a blue-gray preparation. This gray-blue is repeated in the two women above the Virgin, but warmed somewhat by red—now more extensive than originally where the *secco* blue has flaked away. The olive green on the lining of the Virgin's mantle is repeated on the woman alongside her whereas the two Marys who frame the group bear warm colors, one a glorious golden yellow, the other a rich, unusual deep red-brown. All these figures are set off by the white horse, where with very slight variations of tone the painter created a rich surface and a remarkably realistic head. In his palette as well as in his searching description of texture Altichiero recalls his fellow Lombard, Giovanni da Milano (page 98), whose art he must have studied.

In contrast to the Virgin and her attendants, St. John stands erect and a little apart. Though deeply moved, in his bearing and gestures he shows the restraint and the balance of an antique statue.

PISTOIESE MASTER, LATE FOURTEENTH CENTURY, MARY MAGDALEN

Pistoia, San Domenico

★

Though the author of this fresco was not a great painter and we have so far failed to discover his name, he created in this work one of the most poetic images of the century. The Saint appears within a tabernacle, the whole simulating brightly in paint a statue and its canopy. The Magdalen, depicted with extraordinary tenderness, stands in prayer, a penitent in the desert clad only in her own rather glorious golden hair. This simple, natural mantle, surrounded by the rich red of the tabernacle and the frame, seems far more radiant than that of many queens. The Saint forms a striking contrast to the tightly bound Dominican tertiary in black who, as the donor, kneels in adoration below. The Magdalen shows the combination of piety and sensuousness that recurs so frequently in Italian religion and religious art.

The fresco was concealed by new construction in the church in the eighteenth century. It was discovered and detached from the wall in 1958.

STARNINA, BETWEEN 1393 AND 1410, ST. BENEDICT *(overleaf)*

Florence, Santa Maria del Carmine, Chapel of St. Jerome

★

This head and a few other fragments were discovered by Dr. Ugo Procacci in 1932 behind an eighteenth-century wall and then detached and brought to light in 1965. They add essential evidence to the identification of the painter Starnina, to whom Vasari attributed the cycle to which the fragments belong. The evocation of Benedict's blue habit and luminous face and beard prove that Starnina was exceptionally sensitive to the interaction of light and color, and that he thus played an imporant role in the stylistic changes that occurred in early fifteenth-century Florence.

The painting is so strong and the glance so penetrating that we can enjoy the head without being greatly disturbed by its fragmentary character. In doing so we are perhaps aided by our experience with the incomplete forms of contemporary art, from Picasso onward.

LORENZO MONACO, 1422–1425, HEAD OF A PRIEST *(opposite)*

Florence, Santa Trinita, Salimbeni Chapel

For mastery of a linear art among Florentine painters Lorenzo Monaco is second only to Botticelli. In this head all forms—turban, eyelids, mouth and wrinkles—participate in a swirling movement. The painter's brush dances over the surface, curving along the turban and leaving on important lines chains of bright white spots. Though Lorenzo, here working twenty years later than Starnina, was in general a conservative artist, his open brushwork and contrasts of light and dark relate him to major innovations in Florentine painting.

The frescoes in this chapel, badly damaged by dampness, were skillfully restored in 1965. This head is one of the very few rather well preserved surfaces, and these murals are the only ones by the painter that have survived.

PARRI SPINELLI, *ca.* 1445, CRUCIFIXION *(overleaf)*

Arezzo, Palazzo Comunale

★

Parri, son of Spinello Aretino, was the chief painter of the town of Arezzo during the first half of the fifteenth century, and he received the commission for this *Crucifixion* (pages 108–109) from the city. He executed it high on a wall of the main room of the town hall. Though a minor painter, who continued to work in a linear style that had been outmoded in Florence and Siena, he produced for the Comune a striking fresco. It is well preserved except for the loss of the dark blue background, which was applied *a secco*; the visible light blue is the preparatory color. All the forms, painted in a rather unusual monochrome, are in motion: the flamelike rocks, the tall figures swaying like reeds in a breeze, the twisted body of Christ and even the curved members of the green cross.

The disclosure of the preliminary drawing in 1958 when the fresco was detached provided a very agreeable surprise. It is the liveliest monumental drawing by the artist that we have, and indeed even among *sinopie* in general this work has an exceptional animation and sparkle. It gives the impression of great spontaneity, and Parri may actually have worked quickly, for he made many changes in the final composition. There all the postures were changed. The gesture of hand to cheek was given to St. John rather than to the Virgin, and the cross was composed of unplaned logs. Since the fresco shows no signs of a cartoon Parri may have recorded the changes in a small drawing on paper or on a tablet that he brought onto the scaffold while he painted.

The curious monogram scratched into the surface of the fresco and dated 1461 follows a form used for documents by lawyers, one of whom perhaps was responsible for the commission.

MASOLINO, 1424, TWO SAINTS *(following overleaf)*

Empoli, Sant' Agostino

★

These two saints bearing crosses, painted on an arch that opens into a chapel of the Cross, seem to me the best of a surviving group of eight saints and entirely the work of Masolino himself, without the help of assistants (pages 110–111). The concern manifested by Starnina and Lorenzo Monaco with the effect of light on objects (pages 104–105) has led Masolino, the youngest of the three, to conceive of figures that glow with a diffused luminosity. This relatively even distribution of light accords with their graceful movement and gentle, meditative air. In accord, too, are the warm colors and soft textures.

The romantic mood of the figures has been enhanced accidentally by abrasion of the surface, which suggests the weathering effect of time. In some respects, however, the bearded saint is different. Originally, no doubt, his face showed still stronger contrasts of light and dark, a more contracted brow and a sharper glance. These are clear signs of Masolino's attention to the astonishing innovations of the young painter Masaccio (pages 112, 115). After a time every painter in Florence and eventually Europe took account of them, but they were so different from Masolino's own bent that his decision about this time to collaborate with the youthful artistic radical is remarkable.

MASACCIO, 1427 (?), HEAD OF ST. JOHN
Detail of the Tribute Money

Florence, Santa Maria del Carmine, Brancacci Chapel

The alert contemporaries of Masaccio in Florence—and there were many—felt that a new art and architecture of enormous importance had been created in their city in the first quarter of the fifteenth century. The modern world agrees with them. When the great scholar (and later architect) Leon Battista Alberti, who had been living in North Italy and Rome, visited Florence in 1434 he was astonished and delighted by what he saw. To five artists, including one painter, Masaccio, Alberti extended the highest praise he could imagine: their gifts were not inferior, he said, to the most famous of the ancients. They gave him courage about the course of history, because they disproved his belief that the genius of the ancients would never be seen again. "The ability to win fame," he added, "lies in our own industry and diligence no less than in the gifts of nature and the times."

Masaccio's youthful apostle is full of the resoluteness to which Alberti referred. "Men are themselves," Alberti said, "the source of their own good luck and misfortune." The painter joined intelligence and moral strength to compose a figure of unprecedented power. At the same time the poise, the unawareness of the beholder, and even the type of head recall ancient statuary.

The head and the foreshortened halo prove Masaccio's mastery of systematic focus perspective. He had learned the principles from its discoverer, Brunelleschi, and he was the first painter to apply them. Whereas for perspective Masaccio was inspired by an architect, his conception of the figure owed much to sculptors, chiefly Donatello. He struck out largely on his own, however, in his realization of the interdependence of mass and light. Earlier painters modeled all their forms in accordance with a relatively unaltered principle of three regularly graduated areas of value. The source of light, the upper left, was established by convention also, though Giotto in the Arena Chapel and a very few of his followers related it to the main actual source of light in the church.

Masaccio adopted Giotto's scheme in the Brancacci Chapel, but he applied it in a new way. He largely disregarded the example of his predecessors and he painted what his own amazingly intensive analysis had disclosed about the appearance of a particular form at a certain point in space under given conditions of light. As the hand of the apostle shows, he readily sacrificed detailed articulation for a quickly comprehensible, luminous volume.

MASACCIO, 1428, ST. PETER DISTRIBUTING MONEY

Florence, Santa Maria del Carmine, Brancacci Chapel

We know from the history of pictorial style as well as from the words of Vasari that Masaccio's frescoes in this chapel served as a school for painters for a very long time. Taste, however, eventually changes, and in the late seventeenth century they barely escaped replacement by a new decoration; and then in 1771 they were seared by fire. The lower part of this fresco was damaged and repainted (see especially the woman's brown skirt). The entire surface is coated with dirt, and there are many whitish patches of crystallized salt, especially visible in the red robe of St. John. The bright lights of the photographer have penetrated these deposits and disclosed more than is normally visible in the chapel.

Masaccio has represented events described in Acts of the Apostles, when the apostles "distributed to everyone according to his need" the money that had been given to them by the owners of lands and houses, who had sold them for this purpose. Only a certain Ananias held for himself part of the proceeds of his sale, and when his fraud was detected by St. Peter, he fell dead at the apostle's feet.

This story, which exemplifies charity and an egalitarian ideal of Christian communal life, was infrequently represented. It seems as perfect a subject for Masaccio as the scene nearby of Peter healing by his shadow. With his usual stark seriousness the artist re-created both of these events in contemporary Florence, giving to Peter and the unforgettable tragic face behind him features to be seen daily on the Ponte Vecchio. The apostles, attended probably by the donors of money, confront the poor, some of whom are aged and lame. Each group of figures is accompanied by a characteristic building, one wooden, the other a massive stone tower.

These buildings together with the palace at the center rise high above the figures, defining and at the same time closing the space. The street seems to descend behind the people, and then outside the town the slopes of a hill bearing a castle end in very high mountains. The figures, linked by gestures and other means, compose a massive chain that asserts their prominence and maintains their unity in this vast and complex space. The geometric palace frames, and at the same time separates, the two principal figures. Its broad lighted face silhouettes and brings into special prominence the mother and her child.

The light, streaming down from the left as if from the actual window of the chapel, strikes the faces of the apostles and their companions, whereas it falls in little pools on the heads of most of the poor, leaving their faces in shade. The whites of their peering eyes are all the more dramatic.

FRA ANGELICO, *ca.* 1440, TRANSFIGURATION

Florence, San Marco, Friar's Cell

The *Transfiguration* and the *Annunciation* on the following plate are two of forty-one frescoes in the cells of the Dominican friars of San Marco, all by Fra Angelico and his assistants. They compose the most beautiful cycle of monastic paintings of this kind that we know. The chief master was himself a friar in the monastery, and his piety made so great an impression in Florence that his actual name, Guido di Pietro, was soon replaced by Fra Angelico, the angelic friar. The reports about his life merged with the effect of his works to create a legend. In 1550 Vasari wrote that Angelico "never reworked any of his paintings, always leaving them as they had first appeared, because he believed that this was the will of God. . . . He never took up his brush without first saying a prayer."

The unique San Marco cycle is thus the consequence of exceptional circumstances. An unusually pious friar who was also a trained and greatly gifted painter worked for his strict or observant Dominican house that was aided financially and otherwise by the first great Medici patron, Cosimo. The frescoes in the cells, each about six feet high, were intended for quiet contemplation, and Angelico transformed the Christian historical events that he painted into devotional representations. Neither the Virgin Mary nor St. Dominic witnessed the Transfiguration, but the painter introduced them in attitudes of prayer that served as models for the monastic observer.

St. Matthew says that Jesus took Peter, James, and John (who appear in the fresco in that order) onto a mountain. "And Jesus was transfigured before them. And his face did shine as the sun; and his garments became white as snow. And, behold, there appeared Moses and Elias. . . ." At this moment Christ was revealed as the son of God. Fra Angelico gave to this revelation a novel form. Christ spreads his arms in a wide embracing gesture that also forms a cross. He is quite still except for a subtle curl of his drapery along the right and over his foot. The majesty of this unusual figure Fra Angelico owed in large part to Masaccio. Indeed the monastic painter, attentive to the rapid growth around him of a more realistic pictorial style, turned Masaccio's studies of actual light to the realization of a dazzling supernatural event.

FRA ANGELICO, *ca.* 1440, ANNUNCIATION

Florence, San Marco, Friar's Cell

The monastery in which Fra Angelico painted his frescoes had just been built in an early Renaissance style very similar to the architecture he had introduced into his earlier paintings. The San Marco cycle is thus one of the not very common instances of a full sympathy between painter and architect, in this case Michelozzo di Bartolommeo.

In the fresco on the accompanying plate the Annunciation occurs under the graceful cross vaults supported by Ionic capitals that appear in the noble building itself. The scene seems permeated, too, by the stillness of the convent. The angel barely moves. He merely lifts a finger unobtrusively and looks intently at the Virgin. She responds humbly as the servant of the Lord. Though she is exceptionally slight and wears pale colors, the composition culminates in her. The light that streams in from the cloister yard and touches only the skirt of the angel brightens her completely. She is framed and strengthened by the shadow and the door, which assert the vertical axis from which she inclines. The lively cross vaults that unite the two figures curve down close to the Virgin, where they end in capitals; the corresponding forms behind the angel are almost entirely concealed by the wings. Outside the sanctified space St. Peter Martyr, like one of the friars of the convent, stands quietly in prayer. This militant Dominican had been killed by a blow on the head in 1252.

In so spare a design every detail is telling. The fresco, full of the subtlest relations between the human and the geometric shapes, has a sublime simplicity.

MASTER OF THE CHIOSTRO DEGLI ARANCI, 1436–1439,

MIRACLE OF THE RAVEN

Florence, Badia, "Cloister of the Orange Trees"

★

The cycle to which this fresco belongs was painted by a follower of Fra Angelico, probably Giovanni di Consalvo, who had come to Florence from Portugal. The frescoes continued to deteriorate in their open cloister in the Benedictine monastery until they were detached in 1956 and cleaned of earlier repainting except for the linseed oil that had penetrated the colors and still gives them a brown tone.

In the scene reproduced a jealous priest attempts to kill St. Benedict by offering poisoned bread to the monks. This is a minor episode in the life of the Saint, but the painter has known how to transform it into a solemn and important event.

120

In the handsome refectory the monks sit quietly while their abbot, Benedict, sensing the danger, orders a raven to remove the poisoned bread. The Saint, deep in the space, reaches across the table to address the raven with a gesture that is telling, though it lacks perspective or anatomical consistency. The monks at the right are so varied in feature and expression that they strike us as portraits. All but one of the corresponding monks at the left are hidden behind a wall. By this device, which transforms into asymmetry a composition that contains implications of symmetry, the abbot gains prominence and he is put into more immediate relation with the spectator. When, furthermore, the painter decided to make more vivid the depth of the interior by marking its nearer limit, he hung a cloth over the pole at the right, leaving the left open. The cloth, an afterthought, was added in charcoal to the *sinopia*. The painter located the vanishing point for the composition directly below the head of St. Benedict and near his active hand. In this way the new science of focus perspective, introduced only a decade earlier, was immediately employed in the service of the story.

PISANELLO AND ASSISTANT, ARMS OF THE PELLEGRINI FAMILY

Verona, Museum (from Sant' Anastasia, Pellegrini Chapel)

During the first half of the fifteenth century the chief North Italian artist who painted murals was Pisanello. The chapel outside which he executed this shield with a *pellegrino* (pilgrim), emblem of the donor, was completed about the same time as the Florentine frescoes in San Marco and the Badia on the preceding plates. Unlike his Florentine contemporaries, however, Pisanello sought to describe minutely the texture and color of forms. To depict the veins in the pilgrim's hand and almost every single hair in the jacket, the usual dress of pilgrims, he used small brushes that permitted tiny strokes. Such a procedure took time, and he completed much of the work *a secco*. His murals, including the ones in this chapel, have therefore not survived well. This morose, wistful pilgrim is comparatively well preserved, and though perhaps executed by an assistant under Pisanello's supervision, it still conveys the delightful, and in their time famous, accomplishments of the artist.

PAOLO UCCELLO, 1436, MONUMENT OF JOHN HAWKWOOD (*overleaf*)

Fresco, Florence, Cathedral

Preparatory Drawing, Florence, Uffizi

The ancient Romans erected equestrian statues of their emperors, and a few of them survived into the Middle Ages, including the only one that has come down to us today, the statue of Marcus Aurelius on the Capitoline Hill in Rome. These venerable monuments inspired the rulers of several Italian cities to introduce equestrian statues of themselves on their tombs. When wishing to honor successful military leaders whose services they had hired, some cities, particularly Florence and Siena, erected similar statues or simulated them in paint. Uccello's fresco honors the English *condottiere* John Hawkwood, and it celebrates him within the Cathedral of Florence, which began at this time to acquire the character of a pantheon. It is interesting that in shape his horse resembles the famous Hellenistic horses on the façade of San Marco in Venice, where Uccello had been working, for these horses too stood as symbols of a great military victory.

Uccello's painting, nearly thirty feet high, is the first surviving picture that feigns an actual equestrian monument. To develop the illusion the painter constructed the tomb, but not the horse and rider, in accordance with the newly discovered principles of perspective, and he chose a very low point of sight, near the eye of a spectator standing on the floor— one of the earliest instances of such a scheme. According to the perspective the fresco, detached and mounted on cloth, should I believe be placed about five feet higher on the wall than it now is. Indeed the fresco does appear higher on the wall in an unpublished engraving

made before it was detached in 1842. The horse and rider, not included in this perspective scheme, are seen from a conventional position opposite them, presumably to indicate their greater importance.

Though Uccello learned linear perspective and systematic lighting from Masaccio, he wanted to move beyond him by applying geometry not only to the spatial construction but to the forms that appear within it. He gave all his volumes a remarkable regularity. The preparatory drawing shows somewhat more clearly than the fresco the conception of the rump of the horse as part of a perfect circle, and its belly and neck as long arcs.

Uccello probably made several drawings for this large painting. The one in the Uffizi that has miraculously survived represents a final stage in the preparation of the work. It is the earliest drawing we have that shows squares introduced for the purpose of transferring a small composition to a very large one; corresponding squares on the *intonaco* or *arriccio* facilitated the enlargement (see page 126). The drawing is now patched together from two main pieces, and if the lower one, containing the tomb, is moved a little to the right the composition matches the fresco.

In 1550 Vasari criticized Uccello's horse because it moves two hoofs on the same side. Its gait, however, is an amble, common in the fifteenth century on processional occasions and employed again in somewhat later equestrian monuments.

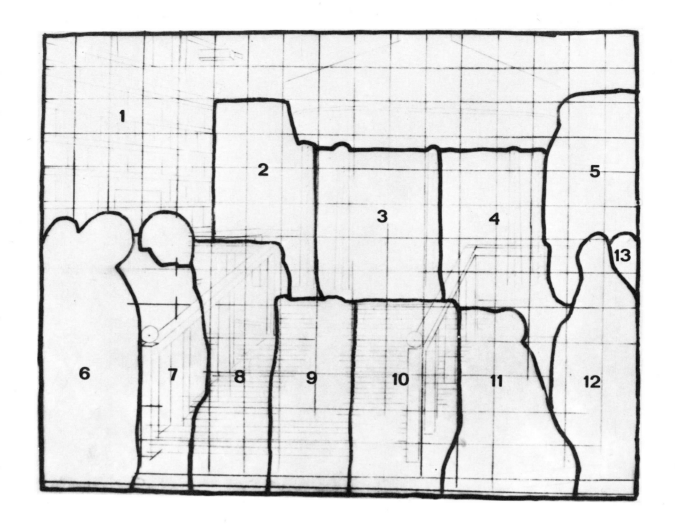

PRATO MASTER, PRESENTATION OF THE VIRGIN IN THE TEMPLE

Prato, Cathedral, Chapel of the Assumption

Two painters were responsible for the frescoes in this chapel: one, Andrea di Giusto, was a mediocre master but the second has been identified with Uccello himself by some historians, although others, including the writer, judge him to be a fascinating assistant and follower. The debate has become more lively since 1964–1965 when the frescoes were cleaned and detached to prevent further deterioration. Only then could we appreciate the full beauty of their bright and often delicious color, their playful geometry and their striking perspective, however unsystematic. In these respects the cycle provides us with precious reflections of the new styles in Florence in the thirties and forties. Of the great innovations during that period by Uccello, Domenico Veneziano, and his pupil Piero della Francesca very little on the large scale of fresco survives.

The Prato Master combines, in a surprising way, geometry and informality. Into his formal setting and amidst ponderous figures he inserts a sprightly little Virgin who sprints up the fifteen steps that, according to the Apocryphal Gospels, led to the temple. A man at the extreme right looks impulsively out of the scene.

The diagram shows the sequence of the daily patches of *intonaco*. The patch containing the head of Joachim, painted after all the adjoining patches, no doubt replaced an original head that proved unsatisfactory. The diagram shows also a system of squares on the *intonaco*, to which they had been transferred from the *arriccio*. The Prato Master had evidently begun with a small squared drawing like Uccello's for the Hawkwood fresco (page 124).

PRATO MASTER, BIRTH OF THE VIRGIN

Prato, Cathedral, Chapel of the Assumption

★

On the wall above the *Presentation in the Temple*, in the lunette formed by the cross vault, the Prato Master painted the *Birth of the Virgin*. It too has been detached, and of the seventy paintings in the exhibition *The Great Age of Fresco* it provided the gayest and most exhilarating color. The Birth had become the scene of much domestic bustle already in the fourteenth century, but nothing approaching the festive occasion envisaged by the Prato Master. Three richly dressed women sweep in to greet the infant and her mother. Their elegance reflects Florentine models by Uccello or Domenico Veneziano, whereas their disproportions and awkwardness, which add a certain provincial charm, were contributed by the eccentric Prato Master himself.

The young woman tripping down the stairs with extraordinary grace, her head-kerchief streaming out behind her and a platter balanced in each hand, is a novel and attractive figure. Her remarkably poised movement is continued even by the women who are seated, for their dresses are tossed about as if they too were dancing. Anne and her servants, much deeper in the space, are smaller in scale, but their variegated green dresses are enlivened by a patterned white wall, a persimmon bedspread, and a flashing white-yellow-brown ceiling. The building is crowned by a zigzag red molding and a large, open, geometric railing. The polished silver pitcher and the transparent glass vases catch and reflect the light.

The painter's intentions seem to waver unpredictably between alternatives, no doubt suggested by artists such as Uccello and Domenico Veneziano who possessed greater assurance. The Prato Master dwells at one moment on line, at another on geometric volume. Several women wear the geometric coiffure characteristic of this period in Florentine painting and, presumably, Florentine life.

The master has a great flair for color. In the pattern of the subtly varied greens and reds the hue of the young woman alongside St. Anne attains the richness of jade, and in the foreground the white dress tinged with rose is delicious. The beautiful twisting arabesques in the frame extend the combination of green and red. Two of the heads in the medallions wear enigmatic expressions, an aspect of the artist's concern that we shall encounter on a larger scale in the following plate.

Prato, Cathedral, Chapel of the Assumption

When St. Stephen sought to convince Jewish elders and scholars of the divinity of Jesus, he met disbelief and anger. This encounter had been represented in the Middle Ages, and in the fifteenth century by Martino di Bartolommeo and Fra Angelico, as a kind of reasonable, academic debate, but in the fresco in Prato the Saint, who points to heaven, is surrounded by a crowd of nine highly surprising characters, who respond in a most unconventional way. The fat man in the detail reproduced rolls his eyes upward, presumably toward heaven, the abode of Jesus as St. Stephen insists, and pooh-poohs the entire conception. The extraordinary young man alongside seems to respond to Stephen with amazement and disbelief.

These astonishing heads prove that the Prato Master had observed intently his contemporaries in the streets of Florence and Prato. It has been suggested, too, that he was influenced by a treatise on physiognomics, the *Secreta secretorum*, ascribed to Aristotle and well known in the fifteenth century. If any artist, however, studied the systematic ideas of this strange treatise Paolo Uccello is the likely candidate. In any event his heads on the clock in the Cathedral of Florence reflect physiognomic interests, and he no doubt influenced the Prato Master in this as in many other respects.

These heads, unique in the entire fifteenth century, remain puzzling in one respect. Did the Prato Master deliberately exaggerate expressions of surprise and scepticism to suggest foolishness and stupidity, or are these faces simply consequences of his own eccentricity? Several heads in the borders of the frescoes wear similar, though less extreme, expressions. We should recall, too, that the painter never got his focus perspective quite straight. He was obviously not given to systematic thought nor indeed to psychological consistency.

Though not endowed with a flair for geometry the Prato Master nevertheless learned enough from Uccello to make an impressive display of it in the black turban and the head it adorns. The repeated circles have, too, a particular function in this context: they make all the more acute the raised brows, the tips of the ears, and the pointed chin.

The attractive, highly individual color of the *Presentation of the Virgin in the Temple* and the *Birth of the Virgin* may be recognized in this detail. Again there are subtle variations of rose and green, including the green underpainting of the flesh. This underpainting remains more exposed in the face of the fat man, because it lies in shade. The light, coming from the left, spreads on part of the face of his companion a soft, creamy warmth.

DOMENICO VENEZIANO, JOHN THE BAPTIST AND ST. FRANCIS

Florence, Santa Croce

This is the best surviving fresco of one of the creators of early Renaissance painting. Vasari admired it sufficiently to save it when in 1566 he demolished the wall around the choir of the church, on which it was painted. It was soaked and damaged, but not seriously, in the flood of 1966.

What might have been a simple composition of two meditative saints standing under an arch became in Domenico's mind a complex, dynamic design charged with strong feeling. For purposes of both realism and increased movement he designed the fresco to be seen from below, so that the spectator is linked to the scheme of divergent glances, up and down, of the saints. Because the point of sight is below the figures, the arch appears to decline and the plane on which the saints stand cannot be seen, depriving them of visible support. Within a plunging spatial tunnel the Baptist is held by the red molding of the arch and St. Francis by the curved outline of the hill and of the far edge of the vault. The figures complement each other, for while the Baptist gazes toward heaven he flings a long arm down and St. Francis looks down while raising his hands in prayer. The saints are highly individualized in physique and in mood, yet perfectly united.

In this fresco, painted in the last decade before his death in 1461, Domenico carried to a new level the analysis of human structure that Donatello had undertaken earlier in stone and bronze. In the figure of the Baptist the artist's searching line and modulated light define the flesh, bones and muscles, from head to toes, in an unprecedented manner. This new realization of high tension in the human body, with all its expressive possibilities, proved important for the entire later Renaissance. The young painter who was most impressed by Domenico's searching analysis, Antonio Pollaiuolo, actually undertook the dissection of corpses in pursuit of anatomical knowledge.

In this late work Domenico retained his very personal, exquisite colors displayed in a soft, flickering light—the rose molding, the gray and buff habit of St. Francis, the white garment of the Baptist delicately shaded in green. In this pattern black acquires a special pungency, and the tousled hair of the Baptist contributes fundamentally to his agitation.

PIERO DELLA FRANCESCA, MARY MAGDALEN

Arezzo Cathedral

For centuries candles burned before this fresco, which covered the wall just to the left of the door to the sacristy. Wax occasionally dropped onto its surface, snuffers scratched it and wicks left black streaks. Yet when these deposits (except some wax) and oxidized modern fixatives were removed in 1963, the painting emerged a little scarred but with more of its original surface intact than any other fresco by the artist.

Like Domenico Veneziano's cult images of the Baptist and St. Francis (page 133), the Magdalen stands under an arch. The point of sight, just below her right hand, is again low, though not nearly as low as Domenico's. Quite apart from its relation to the beholder, the point of sight has a very different function in Piero's design. Whereas Domenico sought oscillation and trans-spatial movement, Piero wanted a great motionless figure looming up above the beholder. She swells to such proportions that she fills almost all the space between the painted piers, and she has a greater volume than the arch itself. At a short distance behind her the recession is closed by a low stone wall.

As often in Piero's compositions, the relation between figure and architecture is symbiotic. The arch restates with geometrical perfection the arc of the saint's shoulders. Proportionately lower, the capitals seem to respond to the horizontal band composed of the vase, the girdle and the fold of the mantle. The fine carved tracery of the arch resembles in delicacy and liveliness the saint's hair. Piero restates in the more abstract mode of white architecture the geometry, proportionality and texture of his figure.

The Magdalen herself has some of the specific qualities of a monument. Her torso is columnar and fluted, all the more striking because the piers are smooth. The imaginative reversal of her mantle reveals a lining as white as the lighted jamb of the arch. The differentiation of the two sides of the figure, of white and red, of vertical and horizontal, heightens her vitality and freedom within the frozen symmetry of the arch.

Though immensely powerful the Magdalen is profoundly still. Her head is turned a little, her eyes cast down, but suggestions of movement seem to be lacking altogether. The combination of boundless vitality and settled immovability is mysterious and bewitching. This is one of the superb icons of all time.

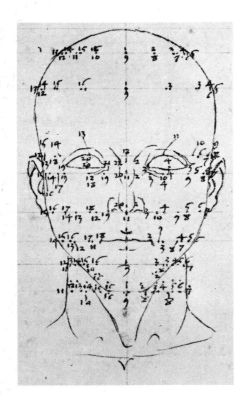

PIERO DELLA FRANCESCA, MARY MAGDALEN
Detail of preceding plate

The Op painter who said the works of Piero della Francesca look like colored postcards need not be taken at his word, but one can appreciate the irritation of many artists of our day with this particular old master. Though Piero now has a very large audience and postcards of his work fly to all corners of the world, the art of no other Renaissance painter seems more remote from the improvisation, the exhibition of unconscious imagery and of the process of creation that are characteristic of our time.

For eloquent proof of Piero's commitment to observation, rational analysis, and mathematical principle one need only look at the line of shade on the Magdalen's neck. The head of the saint is ovoid, and the planes of the face turn with an inexorable regularity and precision. Our sense that the painter was guided by geometry is confirmed by the treatises he wrote. The illustrations for his text on perspective contain drawings of stereometric heads, not unlike the Magdalen's, on which the turning planes are mapped numerically. The aspect of perspective that fascinated Piero most was proportion. All forms in space were subject to a law of relation, *commensuratio* as he said. It is in part the application of this law that gives Piero's paintings their almost magical appearance of finality.

With mathematical principle Piero combines an element of accident and surprise. Wisps of hair curl out unexpectedly from the Magdalen's head. It is fascinating to observe, however, that even such freer forms were partly studied and prepared beforehand in the full-scale cartoon. *Spolveri*, or dots of color, by which the lines of the cartoon were transferred to the *intonaco*, are visible in the hair on the right shoulder.

In other respects too, the painting of the Magdalen, however guided by *commensuratio*, is very unlike a mathematical demonstration. Although the light strikes the forms consistently from the upper left, the brilliant reflections of the lace at the neck, crucial to the entire scale of values, were not of course suggested by any scheme. Piero embodied geometry in unpredictable, luminous color and in variegated texture. The soft, loose hair surrounds a wonderfully sensuous face. The Magdalen has full lips, a rather thick nose, and fleshy cheeks that rise almost imperceptibly to a glow. Only in the world of the flesh would the two eyes be cast asymmetrically.

To measure the degree of all this warmth and softness Piero introduced a chilling contrast, a perfectly regular crystal vase. Though supported only by the saint's fingers, which are strongly foreshortened, the vase is locked into place by the girdle (its final color is lost) and other surrounding shapes. Like the Magdalen it catches and reflects the light, but how icily!

136

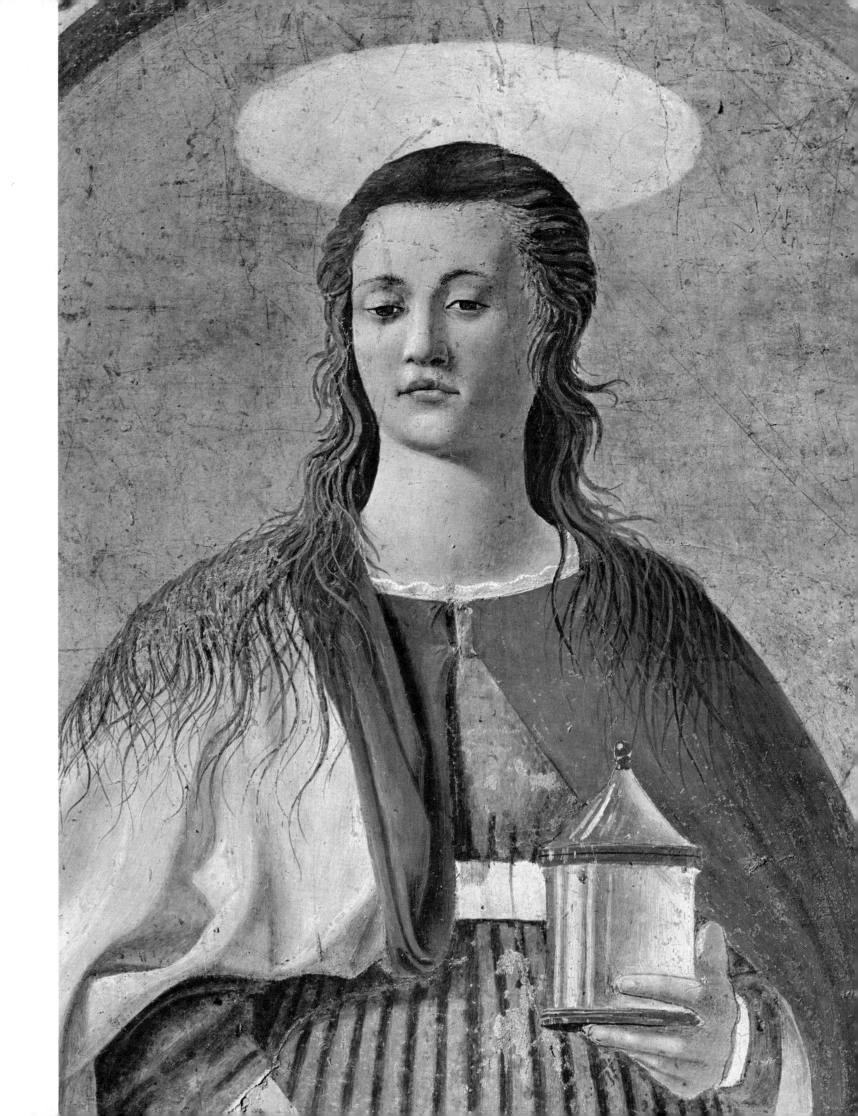

PIERO DELLA FRANCESCA, *ca.* 1460, THE QUEEN OF SHEBA
ADORING THE SACRED WOOD Detail

Arezzo, San Francesco, Choir

The detail reproduced represents one episode in the story of the cross, the chief Franciscan symbol to which the choir in Arezzo, like that in Santa Croce, Florence (page 25), is devoted. The Queen of Sheba, near the end of her journey to King Solomon, recognizes that a piece of wood bridging a stream was destined to be used for Christ's cross, and she drops to her knees to worship it.

Piero, working as a young man in Florence within the shadow of three great predecessors—Masaccio, Uccello, and Domenico Veneziano—managed by his rare genius to compound basic elements of their art in a highly distinctive style of his own. Rather than reject the purposes of his elders he "did Masaccio over again," so to speak, after Uccello and Domenico. He recast the majestic figures of Masaccio in Uccello's geometric mold, and he inserted them in an overall pattern of luminous color developed by his teacher, Domenico. Colors and shapes are interwoven across the surface and simultaneously, though to a lesser degree, in space. The strongest movement, passing through the arms of the attendants to the Queen (and to the vanishing point), courses across the picture plane, but the arms are at different positions in space. The ovoid heads compose a dense design in both dimensions. The more distant heads, intimately related to the nearer ones in tone and shape, nevertheless remain behind them because of overlapping and perspective diminution.

The two aspects of the composition, the planar and the spatial, are held in perfect equilibrium. The saturated red that as always starts out of the painting actually appears on the nearest figure, and it locks into position the saturated blue of the queen. To prevent a strong recession into deep space above the heads of the figures—a recession that would rupture the planar design—Piero introduced a beautiful tree. It spreads over the figures like an umbrella. Its curving branches carry into the sky the curving bodies and arms below it. The undulating heads of the women are echoed in the distance by the outlines of the mountains, which originally, in fact, were more three-dimensional than they appear today.

Most of the attendants of the Queen seem to be one woman wearing different colors and seen from different points of view. For two of them Piero may indeed have used the same cartoon. Their profiles, furthermore, are repeated in simplified form by their white cloth headdresses. Piero has given to these volumes an exceptionally high degree of stereometric abstraction, though of course they remain bathed in luminous color. Late in his life, some twenty years after the painting of this fresco, he wrote a treatise in which he explored the Platonic concept that the whole complex of appearance is reducible to five geometric forms, which have a divine perfection. Here as in his painting he affirmed a belief in a rational world given shape and structure by geometry and number.

PIERO DELLA FRANCESCA, RESURRECTION

Borgo San Sepolcro, Town Hall

Except for *Mary Magdalen*, Piero's frescoes are not well preserved. Already in the fifteenth century the *Resurrection* was moved within the town hall of Borgo San Sepolcro during an architectural reconstruction, and some time after 1700 the fresco was whitewashed. Furthermore, the pigment in the landscape, very probably a green copper acetate, has oxidized and turned brown. In 1550, however, Vasari praised the fresco as the best by the painter in his home town, and it is universally admired as one of his greatest works.

The city of San Sepolcro grew from a shrine containing relics of the Holy Sepulchre, so that the subject of Christ risen from the tomb was a natural choice for a monumental painting in the town hall. Piero conceived the event as occurring behind an opening in the wall framed by two magnificent (painted) Corinthian columns. Christ himself is columnar, and we may recall that other Renaissance artists and theoreticians, following ancient Roman precedent, also associated figure and column as well as head and capital. Piero employed the column and the cylinder repeatedly as basic units in his design of this fresco. Christ's massive, muscular torso is flanked by his staff and his partially cloaked leg. Then, in a chiastic relationship, the slender trees on the right repeat the thin staff, whereas the cylindrical leg at the right is reflected by the stouter trunks at the left.

The lower part of Christ's body is planted approximately at the crossing of two diagonals that extend from the soldiers through the trees. In Piero's complex equilibrium these diagonals extend simultaneously from the lower corners to the opposite upper corners and from the extreme foreground deep into space. Only a structure of such firmness would have permitted the painter so bold a conception as a soldier leaning obliquely out toward the actual space, supported only by his right arm. His real "support" comes from his attachment to the main diagonal and to the geometric shapes around him.

Each of the four soldiers has a distinctive posture, yet they are indissolubly linked with each other. Just as the Queen's ladies (page 138), they seem to open in space like a fan. Their colors are repeated in inverse relation. The soldier at the left wears a rose helmet and a green mantle shaded in violet, whereas the corresponding figure at the right wears a green helmet and a reddish blue jacket shaded in purple.

The soldiers, relaxing in varied, informal postures, are the base and the foil for Christ. He is planted above them, immutable while they are free, absolutely resolute while they sleep, bright where they are dark. His triumphant head looms before the light blue cloud-flecked sky. He is the most inscrutable, the most powerful, the most awesome figure Piero ever painted. The master seems to have brought into Borgo's town hall a Pantocrator from the apse of a Byzantine cathedral—a Pantocrator who retains his distant gaze but is

endowed with the athletic body of an antique Hercules. Physical power is quite clearly an emblem of spiritual might. Some Renaissance artists stated quite explicitly a wish to give the saints a physical beauty similar to that of ancient divinities. Albrecht Dürer, for instance, once said: "Even as the ancients used the fairest figure of a man to represent their false god Apollo we will employ the same for Christ the Lord, who is the fairest of all the earth. . . ."

In a number of late-fifteenth-century paintings the consequences of the Incarnation or Resurrection of Christ are expressed by juxtaposing a bright summer landscape and a lifeless winter one. The Era of Grace follows upon the Era of Old Testament Law. The combination of bare and leafy trees in Piero's fresco has led some historians to conclude that he intended a symbolic meaning of this kind. By tradition, however, the live, regenerated world should be on Christ's right, and until we find a good reason why it should appear here on his left the intention of the painter must remain unclear.

PIERO DELLA FRANCESCA, DREAM OF CONSTANTINE

Arezzo, San Francesco, Choir

This fresco, like all others in the choir (page 138), has been damaged by the infiltration of water and by misguided attempts to "revive" the colors, on one occasion by a good dose of linseed oil. Much of this oil, together with deposits of dirt, salt, and mold, was removed in 1960–1962. This cleaning disclosed Piero's own starry sky in the *Dream* beneath a layer of modern deep Prussian blue. Piero's technical innovations are discussed in the Introduction (page 18), where there is a diagram of the *giornate*, or patches of *intonaco*, of this fresco.

The cones of the tent, repeated in the distance, and the cylinder of the pole are favorite forms of Piero, and so are the opposite, reversed figures of the soldiers. In this fresco, however, which is a little later than the others by Piero (except *Mary Magdalen*) reproduced on the preceding pages, and which was probably painted in the early sixties, the color seems to acquire its own texture and weight.

The *Golden Legend*, a compilation of the late thirteenth century and a major textual source of Piero's cycle, says that when barbarians threatened the Roman Empire an angel appeared one night to the Emperor Constantine and awakened him. When the Emperor looked to heaven he saw a cross formed by a bright light, and on it in letters of gold: "In this sign you will be triumphant." Constantine's vision of victory was no doubt invested with a special meaning when Piero painted it, because only a decade earlier Constantine's city, Constantinople, had fallen to the Turks.

Piero transformed the story significantly. In his principal pictorial model, Agnolo Gaddi's cycle in the choir of S. Croce, Florence (page 25), the cross is a large wooden structure that floats above the circular tent. Piero reduced it to a very small, almost invisible form above the angel's hand. The divine message is carried rather by the light that issues from the angel and floods the Emperor and the forms around him. Furthermore, Agnolo, following the text, showed the Emperor suddenly awakened and looking toward the sign, and the *sinopia*, datable 1424, of Masolino's lost fresco of this subject represents the same dramatic movement.

Piero rejected this established type, drawing perhaps on an earlier tradition, influenced by Eusebius or Lactantius, that showed Constantine asleep. Piero's Emperor lies motionless, his eyes closed but, we infer, his mind open. The artist's mastery of light and color permitted him to envisage a new means of supernatural communication. What had been explicit has become mysterious. The face of the angel who brings light is hidden. We see only the strongly foreshortened, birdlike body that plummets into the space. On the other hand the Emperor and his guards are remarkably still. It is light, the symbol of the spirit, that seems to move. Only ten years later Giovanni Bellini, a student of Piero's work, developed this association of light with the supernatural, and it was indeed Venetian painting that in other respects too made the most of these aspects of Piero's art.

WORKSHOP OF PIERO DELLA FRANCESCA, SAINT JULIAN (?)

Borgo San Sepolcro, Pinacoteca (from Sant' Agostino)

★

This fragment, found in 1957, is the only addition in modern times to the surviving group of frescoes in the style of Piero della Francesca, a very small group except for the choir at Arezzo. Because it was detached from the wall and mounted on a board of compressed wood it could be included in the traveling exhibition of frescoes, and it is reproduced here as one of the most impressive works shown, though it measures only about 4½ by 3½ feet.

So strong were the relationships of geometry, color, and light in the entire original composition, and so completely did they inform every part of it, that the irregularly broken piece that survives retains its strength and contains clear intimations of the whole work. As usual, light and perspective unify the composition. The quite monumental nose throws a large shadow on the cheek, and reflected light from the sleeve turns the adjacent part of the white tunic green.

Impressive though this fresco is, it cannot be considered one of Piero's masterpieces. To a degree the evaluation of it is bound up with the identification of the Saint. If the unusual stare is, as has been suggested, the stunned glance of St. Julian, who murdered his parents, the expression becomes less vacant and more meaningful. It is still true, however, that the relations of the lower edge of the mantle, the sleeve and the white tunic are blunt, and they do not articulate the body in Piero's usual manner. Other forms, such as the rather rigid neck, scarcely bear comparison with Piero's indubitable works, several of which are reproduced on preceding pages.

ANDREA DEL CASTAGNO, *ca.* 1448, CUMAEAN SIBYL

Florence, Sant' Apollonia (from Villa Carducci)

During the Middle Ages the walls of large palaces or town halls frequently bore the images of famous men and women. In France, where there were usually nine of each, called the worthies (*neuf preux* and *neuf preuses*), three were normally chosen from ancient history or mythology, three from the Old Testament, and three from Christian history. The Italian cycles of the fourteenth and fifteenth centuries that we know from literary references depart more or less from this tradition; they reflect both the humanist enthusiasm for ancient history and pride in the great modern writers, Dante, Petrarch, and Boccaccio.

When Castagno undertook to fresco a large room in a villa just outside of Florence, the program included Adam and Eve at the sides of the Madonna, and then on a long wall three recent Florentine military leaders, the three Tuscan literary heroes just mentioned, and between these two groups three heroic women. Whereas all the men are modern these women are not. They belong to the remote past: Queen Esther and Queen Tomyris, liberators of their people, and between them the Cumaean Sibyl. The Cumaean Sibyl, Virgil tells us, dwelt in Italy and her prophecies influenced Roman history, but she appears in Castagno's cycle, as the inscription below her states, primarily because according to a common interpretation of Virgil's *Fourth Eclogue* she predicted the coming of Christ. She therefore points to Heaven while holding a book of prophecies. The diadem set with precious stones and perhaps also the white scarf around her shoulders are attributes of her priestly office.

Like the other worthies in the series, the Sibyl, more than life-size, stands in a niche below a portico (not shown in the reproduction) that is about three feet deep. The plane of the niche on which she stands is invisible because it lies above the point of sight of the perspective. We therefore look up at the Sibyl, as we do at Domenico Veneziano's saints (page 133). In both works the illusion is increased by the projection of the toes forward into, it seems, the actual space we occupy. By giving the warm rose dress highlights in cool, normally recessive, blue Castagno reverses the usual relationship of these colors in a three-dimensional art and creates a tension between them.

The head and neck of the Sibyl, and especially her large hands, show that Castagno shared Domenico's deep interest in structural analysis. On Castagno's figure, however, the highly articulated parts do not function as well as on Domenico's. The hand does not firmly grasp the book, and the arm does not reflect pressure of the hand. Castagno excels in gross anatomy but not in physiology. He gives his figures an overwhelming physical presence—even the Sibyl's hair becomes a mane—but this is usually not equaled by emotional sensibility or moral strength.

CVMANA QVE PROPHETAVIT ADVENTVM

ANDREA DEL CASTAGNO, RESURRECTION

Florence, Sant' Apollonia, Refectory

★

The *Resurrection* and two Passion scenes, all painted by Castagno about 1447, were discovered in 1890 beneath whitewash. The detachment of the badly damaged frescoes in 1953 disclosed powerful, well-preserved *sinopie*. They are also significant historically, for they show the important changes in technique that accompanied changes in style toward the middle of the fifteenth century—changes that were discussed in the Introduction, page 16.

The *sinopia* of the *Resurrection* combines drawings of three very different kinds. The angel is described fully; deep pockets of shade are left by a light that comes from the right rather than the conventional left. On the other hand Castagno drew only the contours of the resurrected Christ. Before indicating these extremities of the figure (the head is not now visible) he must have made a preparatory drawing, probably smaller, on some other surface. The sleeping soldiers are drawn in still another manner. Castagno defined the main volumes with a line of unvarying width; it remains uninterrupted even where the nature of the form changes. The artist was evidently not inventing but recording, and faint spots of charcoal seem to support the inference that he transferred these figures from a full-scale drawing on paper or cloth. The transfer would have been effected by the technique called *spolvero* or dusting, because charcoal was dusted through holes pricked into the lines of the cartoon.

Castagno employed a cartoon for the painting; the *spolveri* visible in Christ and in the soldier at the left leave no doubt about that. The correspondences between the *sinopia* and the fresco are so close that the painter may have re-used one cartoon, or he may have made a second one by tracing from the *sinopia*.

Though it is not easy to judge Castagno's fresco in its damaged state, it does seem to bear the marks of its unusual preparation. The sculpturesque angel seems heavy for the more luminous Christ. Neither the angel nor Christ conform with the stereometry of the soldiers. The additive character of the *sinopia* is thus maintained in the fresco, which does not approach in unity the fresco with which it is always compared: the *Resurrection* by Piero della Francesca (page 141).

ANDREA DEL CASTAGNO, FRESCO, TRINITY AND ST. JEROME
CASTAGNO OR ASSOCIATE, SINOPIA *(both overleaf)*

Florence, Santissima Annunziata

★

St. Jerome, his breast bloody from the stone in his hand, contemplates the Trinity. Alongside him, gazing upward also, are two female saints, one old, the other younger. These saints, variously identified in the past, represent two disciples of Jerome, Paula and Eustochium, her daughter. This novel iconography was no doubt inspired by the new Order of the Hermits of St. Jerome, which was approved by the pope in 1406. They had a lay confraternity near the Annunziata of which the donor of this fresco may have been a member. A later painting by Botticini in London, which came from the original church of the Order in Fiesole, shows Paula and Eustochium, so labeled, alongside Jerome. The image of St. Jerome as penitent, which appeared first in Florence in the early fifteenth century, was also probably inspired by these penitential Hermits.

Since Castagno painted the fresco we would expect him to be the author of the impressive drawing discovered in 1967 beneath it. Certainly it has Castagnesque qualities, such as the weight of the sagging drapery. On the other hand the *sinopia*, which still preserves much of the charcoal that preceded it, is unlike drawings by Castagno that served as definitive models for frescoes, that is, as true *sinopie* (page 150). Perhaps it was intended only as a preliminary full-scale study, to be followed by a cartoon. Still, the figures lack the powerful physical presence that Castagno normally gave them.

Instead of the haggard old man in the fresco, his toothless mouth open, his bony body exposed almost to the midriff, the drawing shows a lithe, agile saint looking toward God with hope, one hand extended to balance his movement as in figures by Domenico Veneziano. The fresco greatly heightens the pitch of emotion by agitated drapery, staccato projections, and by the addition of a lion whose rolling eye and gaping mouth echo those of the saint.

Whoever executed the elaborate drawing, Castagno decided to alter the design and proceeded to draw a full-scale cartoon. The *spolveri* of the cartoon can be seen clearly in the detail of the head.

Even after completing the fresco the master did not stop. He felt dissatisfied with part of the Trinity, which had not been explicitly indicated in the drawing. Wishing to transform symbols into full corporeal and perspective reality Castagno, like some other early Renaissance painters, occasionally got into trouble. He painted the lower part of Christ's body in drastic and, as it proved, quite awkward foreshortening. This he decided to conceal. Over the loincloth and the legs he painted seraphim. Since he made this addition *a secco* the paint as usual has peeled, so that today we can again detect, and indeed sympathize with, the sources of Castagno's discontent.

BENOZZO GOZZOLI, TABERNACLE OF THE VISITATION Detail

Castelfiorentino

★

Of the countless wayside shrines that existed in medieval and Renaissance Italy only a relatively few survive, and then often without their paintings. The lower frescoes on Gozzoli's tabernacle that stood on the road from Castelfiorentino to Volterra were washed away by floods of the nearby river Elsa, and a leaky roof led to the destruction of part of the uppermost frescoes. To preserve what was left the paintings, still very bright, were detached in 1965 and remounted on sheets of masonite that had been given the exact form of the tabernacle, over thirty feet high.

The tabernacle was dedicated to the Virgin, and the distribution of the scenes follows a common pattern. The angel Gabriel and the Annunciate Virgin appear in the spandrels of the arch, while God the Father hovers above. Within the arch at the lower level there was a frescoed altarpiece of the Madonna enthroned and saints; only the heads and the entablature remain. Above, in the scene of the Expulsion of Joachim, the painter constructed a deep temple, the more distant vault of which echoes the actual arch of the shrine.

Since the painter wished to preserve the round shape of the arch the space in the frescoes on its inner face is shallow. The surface is largely filled by a figure of Christ encircled by seraphim above the Evangelists and Fathers of the Church. The visible figures, Matthew and Gregory as well as Mark and Jerome, sit on banks of clouds before a cloud-streaked sky. The frosty clouds approximate in texture the simulated capitals. These forms add to the even distribution over the entire surface of bright color and starchy texture that is part of Gozzoli's gaiety and charm.

ANDREA MANTEGNA, 1454, DECAPITATION OF ST. JAMES   Destroyed

Padua, Church of the Eremitani, Ovetari Chapel

The ektachrome on which this reproduction is based was one of those taken in March 1944, a few days before a stray bomb destroyed the chapel and its frescoes. Two damaged scenes that had been detached years earlier were stored elsewhere and saved, but the loss to art was perhaps the greatest of the Second World War. By good luck the color separation films of this fresco, made for a publication of 1945, have been preserved, and it has been possible to produce a far more faithful reproduction now because of the improvement in color-printing since that time. We can see that before the destruction the strong greens, orange-yellows and brick reds of Mantegna's early style were well preserved, though the blue applied *a secco* in the upper area of the sky had flaked off and disturbed the pattern of color by disclosing the red preparatory painting below it.

The decapitation of the apostle, about to be accomplished by an unusual small guillotine instead of by sword, occurs in the immediate foreground, very close to us. The brutal executioner expends such force in raising the huge mallet that he rips his tunic. Near this scene of violence a soldier leans casually over a fence. The supervising officer, elegantly dressed and curbing his beautifully rendered horse, meditates upon the event.

Most of the fresco is devoted to a hill that rises steeply from the shallow foreground, creating the most impressive effect of size and distance that had yet been realized in Renaissance painting. This stony mountain distracts us from the scene of martyrdom, but the twisting road and the bands of vegetation, which create a sense of rotation, add to the tense excitement of the event. The rent garment of the executioner, furthermore, is echoed by similar jagged cracks in the buildings. One branch of the tree, too, has a sharp break.

The ruins, like those of Maso di Banco (pages 62–63), no doubt allude to the decline of the pre-Christian world, but Mantegna, the first great antiquarian painter, gave them (as well as the soldiers) a far more specifically Roman form. For him these decaying structures were not, however, simply signs of a waning paganism but also, and paradoxically, symbols of a glorious artistic past that he strove to recreate.

Mantegna's perspective, though based on the system invented and applied in Florence (pages 125 and 133), contains striking innovations. The declining plane of the nearest foreground shows that he identified the point of sight with the eyes of the spectator standing in the chapel and thus a little below the fresco. The vivid sense of perspective actuality created by this design is increased by the depiction of some forms as if they existed not in the illusory pictorial world but in the real space of the spectator. The wooden fence seems to be in it, attached as it is to the front surface of the frames of the fresco (not shown); and since the soldier leans over this fence he moves out still further toward us into the space of the actual chapel.

ANDREA MANTEGNA, 1472–1474, LANDSCAPE   Details

Mantua, Ducal Palace, Camera degli Sposi

Twenty years after painting the *Decapitation of St. James* Mantegna designed another landscape, softer but more fantastic. In it he set a large, natural aperture of rock, which frames a distant hill-town. He clearly continued to be fascinated not only by Rome and the remote in time but by the distant in space. He liked the direct, poignant contrast of Duke Lodovico Gonzaga's horse and squire in the foreground with the tiny figures, now indistinct, that move over the hill toward the natural arch or the masons on the scaffold who complete the battlements of the tower. Though describing with a miniaturist's precision the details of the landscape Mantegna gave powerful volume and movement to the great, eruptive masses, creating the most fanciful and imposing mountain scenery of the fifteenth century.

The painting, executed in a mixed technique related to that of Piero della Francesca (page 18), begins a series of views of the Gonzaga court. The episodes are revealed by the lifting of painted curtains that hang from poles extending between fictive pilasters.

ANDREA MANTEGNA, 1472–1474, CENTER OF CEILING

Mantua, Ducal Palace, Camera degli Sposi

Mantegna maintained in the ceiling of the Camera the illusionism of the walls. For centuries painted vaults and ceilings had been associated with heaven or the sky. Giotto covered the barrel vault of the Arena Chapel with stars and a few roundels that enclose sacred figures (page 43). Similar figures, now seated on clouds, appear in the arch of Gozzoli's tabernacle (page 157). Employing perspective for an effect like that created by the rocky aperture (page 160) Mantegna dissolved the center of the ceiling, transforming a roundel into a light well and a parapet that opens onto a bright sky. Three *putti* standing inside the parapet, drastically foreshortened, are seen in a surprisingly unconventional way. Others poke their heads inquisitively through openings in the fence. An orange-tub, projecting from the parapet, is balanced, a little threateningly, on a wooden pole. While we look up at this attractive vista several smiling women look down into the room. All of this promotes a sense of rapid movement through space, which enhances greatly the credibility of the illusion: enhances it, but does not really make it quite credible. Mantegna invites us to join him in a gay game of make-believe, and he persuades us that the experience is entirely delightful.

FRANCESCO DEL COSSA, 1470, VENUS AND HER "CHILDREN" *(overleaf)*

COSSA OR ERCOLE DEI ROBERTI, A DECAN IN AUGUST *(opposite)*

Ferrara, Palazzo Schifanoia, Hall of the Months

In the third quarter of the fifteenth century the ruling Este family transformed Ferrara into a major cultural center. They attracted to their city the greatest artists within Italy, such as Piero della Francesca, and even from the North, such as Roger van der Weyden. Inspired by these models and by the general cultural renewal, three local painters, including Francesco del Cossa and Ercole dei Roberti, gave the Ferrarese school European prominence and an elaborate, quite distinctive kind of fantasy.

Of the many frescoes the Este commissioned for their new buildings only part of a cycle of the Months in the Palazzo Schifanoia survives. The program, devised by the court astrologer, reflects the great influence of this pseudo-science on contemporary Italian life. Horoscopes sent men into battle, delayed treaties, and launched ships. In the Schifanoia cycle one of the twelve great Olympian deities reigns over each month: in Cossa's fresco Venus over April. In the zone below each planet appear the zodiacal sign of the month and three decans, one for each ten days. The last ten days of August are controlled by the woman often ascribed to Cossa but painted, I believe, by Ercole dei Roberti.

Alongside Venus in Cossa's fresco are the men and women born in this month who are subject to her influence—lovers all, suffused with quiet happiness. Even the few who are amorously engaged act with a certain ceremonial grace. The strains of music stir their feelings and exalt their mood. The air is fragrant with the scent of fruit and flowers, and one man contemplates a carnation given him by a companion. These enchanted young people are accompanied by rabbits, prolific creatures traditionally associated with the goddess.

Venus, like the other deities, assumes the attributes given to her in the medieval mythographic tradition. Swans draw her float and doves flutter near her. She wears contemporary dress, her head is encircled by red and white roses, and she holds a shell in one hand, flowers in the other. At her feet kneels Mars, tamed and in chains. Whereas Mars and Venus appear here in medieval, chivalric guise the Three Graces at the upper right have reassumed their antique composition. These nude figures are one of the first examples in Renaissance art of a mythological subject restored to its ancient form.

The bumpy bodies of the Three Graces, to be sure, are not unaffected by the fanciful eccentricity that informs the entire composition. From the flat planes of the silvery water and the delicate green terrain, fantastic crags erupt suddenly. Venus is framed by violet stalagmites, and the red lappets of her barge flutter stiffly in the breeze.

Ercole dei Roberti painted more fluently than Cossa even here in the decan for August when he was just emerging from Cossa's workshop. The cleaning that has just been completed reveals this figure as one of the most beautiful fragments in the cycle, unforgettable for its posture, its rippling movement, and its rare and precious color.

REDDE NOS [C]LAROS LAMPAS RADIO
SINE QVA TERRA TOTA EST FVMBROSA

DOMENICO GHIRLANDAIO, 1480, ST. JEROME

Florence, Church of Ognissanti

This fresco, dated 1480 by an inscription on the desk, and Botticelli's *St. Augustine*, reproduced on the following plate, were painted on the wall of the old monks' choir; they confronted one another on opposite sides of the door that led into the choir from the nave. Vasari says that the two painters, working at the same time, tried to outdo each other. When the monks' choir was demolished in 1564 sections of the wall bearing the frescoes were moved to their present positions on opposite sides of the nave—early instances of the transportation and salvage of frescoes. The floodwaters of 1966 added to earlier losses in the lower areas of both paintings (see page 9), and in the spring of 1969 they were detached. Since the photographs were taken soon after detachment, they show white plaster that had not yet been toned down in the course of restoration.

A book on St. Jerome written in the fourteenth century by a professor of canon law at the University of Bologna was largely responsible for the popularity of images of the saint as a scholar in his study. In the profusion of professional paraphernalia Ghirlandaio far outdid his presumed model, even though that was designed and partly painted by a great master of still-life, Jan van Eyck, whose panel of St. Jerome belonged to the Medici in Ghirlandaio's time. The objects are distributed in the very limited space with an impressive logic and economy. Even the edges of the shelves hold a rosary, extra ink, and a sort of motto in largely legible Greek taken from a Psalm. The eyeglasses, the black and red ink (the Saint has splattered a little), the scissors, rule and candlestick, all have their proper places fixed to the desk or set on the rich fifteenth-century Anatolian carpet. In addition to Latin manuscripts the shelves bear proof of Jerome's linguistic proficiency, not only in Greek but in Hebrew, some lines of which Ghirlandaio has copied carefully but uncomprehendingly on a scroll. On the upper shelf it would be difficult to add one more vase, box, faïence *albarello*, or piece of fruit—unless the cardinal were to put on his hat.

Inspired by the Eyckian oil painting, Ghirlandaio has described with equal brilliance in fresco the color, shape, and texture of all the objects and their relation to the light that flows in from the right. Yet all turns on the Saint. He catches most of the light, throws the largest shadow, and has the most free space. He looks insistently at the beholder, whose point of sight is unusually close and at the level of his eyes.

BOTTICELLI, *ca.* 1480, ST. AUGUSTINE

Florence, Church of Ognissanti

Whereas in 1550 Vasari remarked about the *St. Jerome* that Ghirlandaio surrounded the scholar with an "infinity of instruments and books," he said Botticelli's *St. Augustine* showed that profound meditation and penetrating subtlety that appears only in persons devoted continually to the investigation of the highest and most difficult things. Whereas Ghirlandaio used every means to give the spectator a sense of intimacy with St. Jerome, St. Augustine, seen from a much lower point of sight, is rapt in a vision of the supernatural, symbolized in part by the golden rays that descend toward him. Perhaps it is the moment described in an apocryphal text when Augustine, beginning to write a letter to Jerome, by chance at the moment of his death, hears his voice describing the glory of Heaven. Jerome tells Augustine to curtail his attempts during his earthly life to understand God; indeed, he says, the heavens would sooner cease their motion than the Saint would, before death, comprehend eternal bliss. Perhaps in part for this reason an armillary sphere appears in the fresco behind the golden rays, and a text on geometry stands open behind a clock, symbol of finite time. The clock bears the "counterclockwise" numerals of Uccello's clock of 1443 and other early timepieces. The blue in Botticelli's clock, incidentally, shows us the quality of the common pigment azurite near the very costly, slightly reddish lapis lazuli used for the cover of the book on the shelf.

The golden rays are accompanied by a beautiful, cool natural light that, as in Piero's *Dream of Constantine* (page 144), falls principally on the Saint and seems to fill him with an unearthly grace. Botticelli employs light also to stress the edges of the tense forms of the face and the hands. Reflected light increases these effects in the fingers.

Not everything in the fresco rises to this level of solemnity. The conspicuous red and blue shield of the Vespucci family on the frieze refers to the donor (perhaps of the *St. Jerome* also), probably the father of the great navigator, Amerigo. Though in the geometrical treatise most of the script is scribble, three lines contain letters that have become clearly legible since the recent cleaning. "Where is Friar Martin? He has vanished. Where has he gone? He is outside the Prato Gate." This gate is not far from the church, and beyond it the friars of Ognissanti, the Umiliati, possessed property. What the prominence given to Friar Martin's disappearance may signify, I leave to future historians.

The rather carelessly written inscription in the frieze, added after 1564 when the fresco was moved, shows something of the same playful spirit." Augustine has devoted himself so completely to sacred studies that he is still not aware that his location has been changed." Until recently the frieze of *St. Jerome* bore a similar inscription: "St. Jerome, so that your image woul dlack nothing, recently—wonderful to behold—motion was given by art [the technique of transfer?]." This inscription has been cleaned off, disclosing the handsome original epigraph, taken probably from an old hymn to St. Jerome.

PERUGINO AND PINTORICCHIO (?), 1481, CHRIST PREACHING
AND BYSTANDERS Detail of the Baptism

Vatican, Sistine Chapel

At the beginning of the decoration of his new chapel Pope Sixtus IV gave Perugino the principal role. This Umbrian master trained in Florence painted the altarpiece as well as the Birth of Christ and the Finding of Moses on the altar wall, and he undertook also at least the design of the first scene devoted to the life of Christ, the *Baptism*. Some, but not all, historians believe Pintoricchio executed most of the fresco; the style of the two young painters was so close at this time that distinctions are difficult.

The photograph here reproduced was taken from the scaffold just after restorers had completed the cleaning of the fresco. They were able to remove some but not all of the oil applied as early as the eighteenth century, disclosing far more of the original color than has been visible for at least a century. The cleaning of the rest of the cycle in the chapel will probably throw new light on the problems of authorship.

In the detail reproduced we see Christ after the Baptism, standing on a hill above the River Jordan and delivering his first sermon. Most of the men and boys below look toward the Baptism. Almost all of them are portraits, brilliantly yet coolly rendered. They are no doubt persons connected with the Curia. Despite the solemnity of the moment a young man fingers the golden chain of the main figure, who is frequently but incorrectly identified as the brother-in-law of the Pope. The representation of contemporaries of the donor as witnesses of the great Christian events had begun to become common in the third quarter of the fifteenth century; in the Sistine Chapel their number constitutes a major invasion.

The foliage and the rocks around Christ sparkle with golden reflected lights. The use of gold for luminosity had been rejected by the main Renaissance pictorial tradition from Masaccio to Piero della Francesca, and it was condemned by the theorist Alberti. It was revived, however, by their successors, above all by the Umbrian masters, especially for the representation of highlights. The display is especially scintillating in the Vatican frescoes, beginning with the Sistine Chapel. It is accompanied by a greater richness of dress and a new aristocratic bearing. Even Christ's mantle is fastidiously disposed, and when addressing the populace he crooks the little finger of his gesturing hand.

DOMENICO GHIRLANDAIO AND WORKSHOP, 1484–1486, PALAZZO VECCHIO   Detail of the Approval of the Franciscan Rule

Florence, Santa Trinita, Sassetti Chapel

Domenico Ghirlandaio, who had worked alongside Perugino and Botticelli in the Sistine Chapel in 1482, returned with them to Florence late in that year to execute a commission in the Palazzo Vecchio or town hall. Then he and his assistants undertook to paint the chapel of the great merchant Francesco Sassetti in the church of S. Trinita, and in one of the frescoes, here reproduced, he represented the building in which he had just been employed.

Francesco Sassetti's patron saint was Francis, and since the Dominicans of Sassetti's church objected to the representation of the founder of the rival order Sassetti commissioned a cycle of scenes for a chapel in S. Trinita. One of these scenes, in a lunette below the vault, shows at its center Pope Honorius approving the rules of the Franciscan Order. The important event occurred, as everyone knew, in Rome, but the influential donor decided to locate it in the main square of his own city, surrounding the ecclesiastics with Florentine buildings, including the town hall that appears in the accompanying plate.

After the fresco was painted Sassetti took an even bolder step. He had parts of the *intonaco* cut out so that portraits of himself, of Lorenzo de' Medici and their families could be inserted in the foreground. One of these added portraits, painted on a crudely inserted patch of plaster, appears in the lower left corner of the plate. The tonsured man behind him, who seems at that time to have been painted out, is again visible. The photographer's raking light reveals clearly also the incisions the painter ruled into the damp plaster to define the main lines of his buildings.

Ghirlandaio shows us one of the most famous corners in the world as it looked in his day. Of course the Uffizi, begun by Vasari for the Medici in 1561, did not yet exist. Instead we see a cluster of buildings, including (just behind the Palazzo) a strip of the façade of the eleventh-century church of S. Pier Scheraggio. Some frescoed columns of the nave of this church still survive and are visible at the entrance to the Uffizi Gallery.

The parapet of the Palazzo Vecchio is provided with hooks and rings for flags and cloth hangings. On a pedestal rests a gilded statue of a lion or *marzocco*, the symbol of a free Florence. Two more lions appear over the door. Some years later, in 1504, an even better known symbol of Florentine freedom was placed at this door: Michelangelo's *David*. A Cistercian friar leans out of a window; he is probably one of the members of this Order who kept the municipal keys and seal.

BOTTICELLI, 1482, THE TRIALS AND TRIUMPH OF MOSES

(preceding plate)

The Vatican, Sistine Chapel

Few if any works of art would look effective below Michelangelo's ceiling, and until the fifteenth-century frescoes on the walls of the chapel began to be cleaned three years ago they seemed gray and dull, though they are each about eighteen feet long. Paintings of this period, indeed, suffer more than later paintings from deposits of dirt and discolored "restorations" because so much of their character, even as stories, resides in bright, subtly varied color and crisp detail. We are reminded of the dead opacity of Botticelli's delicate, luminous sky and water before cleaning by the small square patch of dirty sky the restorers have left to the right of the crown of the tree. The cleaning has furthermore transformed the dun frames into sparkling architecture, and, astonishingly enough, it has disclosed under nondescript paint in the frieze the handsome majuscules of the original titles, impressive examples of the newly revived Roman imperial epigraph. In Botticelli's fresco the title reads "The perturbation of Moses, bearer of the written law." The monumental inscription seems especially appropriate because it appears above a portrait of the Arch of Constantine, in general faithful except for the stones heaped on the attic to prove its non-Christian antiquity.

As a program for the two long walls of his new chapel Pope Sixtus IV selected the authority of the Church, to be exemplified by scenes on the north wall from the life of Christ and on the south wall by episodes from the life of Moses. The fifth scenes, opposite each other, represent Christ's gift of the keys to St. Peter, and in Botticelli's fresco, the Lord's support of Moses and his priest Aaron. Botticelli has emphasized Aaron's similarity to Peter by giving him a sort of blue and gold papal tiara.

On the arch of the first Christian emperor the epigraph, taken from Hebrews (5:4), states that only those, such as Aaron, who are chosen by God may serve as priests. Aaron censes undisturbed behind the altar whereas Moses, who raises his staff, condemns the unauthorized priests to sudden attack by the flames of their own censers (Leviticus 10:1–2). The other two episodes are difficult to identify because they are rarely represented and the Bible is complex. At the right Moses, his arms raised, appears to escape from an attempted stoning by disgruntled Israelites (Numbers 14:6–9. Christ is stoned in the fresco opposite). In the left corner two rebels are swallowed up by the earth before Moses, while two young men who are saved float on a cloud (Numbers 16:29–33; 26:9–11). These threats to priestly authority no doubt allude to a challenge to the power of Sixtus IV.

Botticelli was the greatest painter who worked on this cycle, but his genius was not perfectly suited to the celebration of papal power. He succeeded in conveying the destruction of the enemies of the priesthood but not its enduring strength. The arch is impressive but Moses, despite his vigor, is less so. He remains passionately involved in passing events.

Florence, Santa Maria Novella, Strozzi Chapel

Abraham is one of the four Old Testament patriarchs who appear commonly in Florentine art of the fifteenth century, but Jacob is not, and perhaps for this reason he alone is not simply named (the inscription not visible) but also given a scroll. On it is written "This is the house of God and the gate of heaven" (Genesis 28: 17). Jacob spoke these words after his vision of the heavenly ladder, and the marble bowl in his hand may refer to the container for the oil he poured on the stone on which he had slept during this vision (or it may be the bowl of venison used to deceive his father). Jacob looks into a book held open by angels.

The frescoes were commissioned in 1487 by a member of the patrician banking family, Filippo Strozzi, and since the contract leaves to him the choice of figures in the vault, he may have preferred Jacob to the usual symbol of republican ideals, David, who is not represented. The contract requires the painter to work "in fresco," perhaps the first instance of such a stipulation. This Filippino did, though the lapis lazuli, the high quality of which was fixed in the contract, may have been applied *a secco*. Traces of this fine blue are still visible around the top of Jacob's scroll. The soft green, somewhat worn, is malachite and the rich red in both frescoes is cinnabar.

All this marvelous color, subtle and subdued in *Jacob*, brilliant in *Abraham*, has been disclosed by a cleaning completed in the fall of 1969 just before the ektachromes were made. These patriarchs are part of Filippino's major late mural cycle, full of streaming forms. Every object, whether animate or not, has a vitality of its own. Indeed the carved heads at the base of the altar seem almost alive, certainly by contrast with the limp sacrificial lamb above. Abraham, magnificently overcharged, is the most theatrical figure of the century. He sits amidst clouds and violet seraphim, still quivering from the narrow escape of his only son and pondering the words of the Lord.

LUCA SIGNORELLI, 1500–1504, PORTRAITS OF HIMSELF AND OF FRA ANGELICO (?)   Detail of History of Anti-Christ

Orvieto, Cathedral, Chapel of San Brizio

On the walls of this large chapel Signorelli represented the end of the world, the Resurrection, the Blessed and the Damned, and the history of Anti-Christ, of which a detail is reproduced. In the vast space opened by the painter Anti-Christ tries to deceive Christians by preaching, by false miracles, and by rebuilding the Temple of Solomon. If all these fail, he inflicts physical punishment, including the cutting of throats. Strangulation and death are represented in the foreground of the detail. In the background lie the followers of Anti-Christ, smitten by the Archangel Michael. Perhaps the depiction of these events on so grand a scale was influenced by the tumultuous career of Savonarola and his downfall in 1498.

At the extreme left edge of the fresco, close to the architectural forms that frame it, stand two men. Their separation from the scene is enhanced by their black dress, a color unique in an area of pale blue, rose, and brown. The younger man points, in a rather detached way, at the events nearby; the other, clasping his hands, has the intent outward glance that is characteristic of self-portraits, which were normally executed by the use of a mirror. Vasari said that Signorelli painted himself in this cycle, and since the master was about 50 to 55 years old in 1500 all the evidence supports the identification.

Half a century before Signorelli, Fra Angelico had begun the painting of the chapel, and the younger man, a Dominican, is now universally regarded as a portrait of him, though the identification was made some time after Vasari, and no existing portraits of the painter confirm it. As a precedent, however, for the depiction of a colleague alongside a self-portrait, we may recall Ghiberti's reference to Taddeo Gaddi's painting of Giotto and himself.

The two men act as intermediators, Signorelli attracting our eye and his companion leading us into the scene. It is tempting to suppose that when Signorelli envisaged these two figures he had in mind Virgil and Dante as visitors to Hell, especially because in the Chapel he painted portraits of these two poets surrounded by scenes from Dante's *Purgatory*.

Of course Signorelli and the putative Fra Angelico belong to that category of contemporaries more or less involved in religious events that we have encountered in Perugino's *Baptism* (page 173). The fact that these bystanders are well-dressed painters shows how much the social position of artists and the general estimate of their work had changed from the time before Giotto, when they were regarded simply as craftsmen. Painters now were the objects of biographies and autobiographies; in art they assumed positions normally given to donors and their families or friends. Half a century earlier Alberti, the great champion of artists and student of Pliny, had written that painting contains a divine force not only because it makes absent men present but the dead almost alive.

FRA BARTOLOMMEO, ST. FRANCIS EMBRACING ST. DOMINIC

Florence, Pian di Mugnone, Convent of the Magdalen

★

This lunette, painted above an exterior door, was the most damaged fresco in the exhibition. It was nevertheless one of the most moving, so simple and expressive are the postures of the figures. Fra Bartolommeo painted the fresco in the last years of his life, which ended in 1517.

The two great mendicant orders, the Dominicans and the Franciscans, did not always live side by side peacefully and with affection (see page 175). Many friars in both Orders, however, sought a relationship that was best symbolized by an embrace of the two founders. Of all the images of St. Francis and St. Dominic together, this worn fresco by Fra Bartolommeo, himself a Dominican friar, is perhaps the most beautiful. He painted it for the monastery, which was a Dominican hospital, probably while he was recovering from an illness.

SODOMA, 1505–1508, ST. MAURUS TREADING ON WATER

Monteoliveto Maggiore (Siena), Great Cloister

Detail (overleaf)

Sodoma was clearly only a minor painter in the early sixteenth century. Nevertheless, fired by the great artists around him and by the enthusiasm for painting felt throughout the peninsula, he occasionally rose to enchanting poetic heights.

The quality of this fresco, extremely delicate as it is, could scarcely be perceived when it was still in the open cloister, damaged by exposure to the weather. Detachment and cleaning in 1969 revealed a painting of captivating luminosity. Sodoma, guided by Leonardo da Vinci and Perugino, whose works he had studied carefully, learned how to provide an engaging equivalent for natural beauty, for earth, trees, water, and a pale sky streaked with clouds tinted by a setting or rising sun. He used only a few pigments, including a superb blue in the water that has just now been identified as smalt, which contains cobalt. In various combinations these pigments suffice for the depiction of the Benedictines too, who become part of the landscape.

Sodoma has conjured up his world with great affection, delighting in the evocation of eddies in the river, shadows under the bridge, or a rivulet splashing down from a grassy mound. The tall tree is given an almost Chinese refinement and animation. The space is deep and mysterious. The sky seems to change as we watch it.

St. Maurus is shown responding to the call of his abbot, Benedict. Setting out to rescue a fellow monk who is in danger of drowning, Maurus succeeds by walking, miraculously, on the surface of the water.

MICHELANGELO, 1511, DANIEL   Detail of Ceiling

Rome, Vatican, Sistine Chapel

For the ceiling of the Sistine Chapel Michelangelo, like his predecessor Giotto (page 43), devised a series of frescoed arches that sweep across the vault. Michelangelo's arches rise from the wall between the windows and the lunettes just above them, as the accompanying plate shows. At the beginning of each of these girders, as it curves away from the wall, he placed a prophet or a sibyl. They are seated on stone thrones, the two vertical sides of which continue as ribs across the vault. Like a good Florentine, Michelangelo has kept in mind the law of gravity, placing the heavy forms of the seers above the walls rather than over the windows.

The prophets and sibyls are enormous, their height even when seated approximating the height of an entire scene of the life of Christ or Moses on the wall below (page 176). Gigantic images had sometimes appeared in the apses or on the walls of medieval churches, but Michelangelo's array is really unprecedented. Of course we are impressed less by the actual than by the *apparent* size of these figures. The painter indeed increased the effect of bulk and power as he proceeded along the ceiling from the entrance door to the altar. The first prophets and sibyls, though huge, fit into their allotted spaces whereas Daniel, in the last group to be painted, breaks out of his space at both sides and for the first time a head rises into the enframing architecture above. With great verve he leans far off center to record—presumably one of his prophesies—on a little desk. The vertical axis is restored by two small figures, who are connected with Daniel's creativity. One, nude and very active, supports the heavy book which the prophet consults. The other, mysterious in a violet cloak before the lighted stone, seems to embody the spirit of discovery.

Only Michelangelo could weave together such disparate forms into an incessantly swaying group, and yet maintain absolute equilibrium and order. And certainly only he could see and realize in one image both the intensely bright and solid and the disturbingly dark and ineffable.

The two pairs of gray putti were painted from one cartoon, used in reverse. Their play here seems to verge on strife. The photographer's lights, perhaps a little too bright, take us, so to speak, behind the scenes. They reveal vividly that this unique masterpiece suffers from discolored repaint applied in the past, from altered fixatives, and even from the recent flaking of pigment. This fresco and Michelangelo's *Last Judgment* are the only ones in such a state that are reproduced in this book.

DANIEL

RAPHAEL, 1511–1514, LIBERATION OF ST. PETER FROM PRISON *(overleaf)*

Rome, Vatican, Stanza d'Eliodoro

On a visit to Rome in July 1512 Alfonso, Duke of Ferrara, climbed the scaffold in the Sistine Chapel to look with Michelangelo at the ceiling that would soon be completed, but when his hosts then suggested he see what Raphael was doing in the papal apartments he declined the invitation. If he had gone he would have found the painter working in the room that contains the *Liberation of St. Peter*, for which Raphael had made a drawing probably in 1511.

According to the Acts of the Apostles (12:3–11) Peter, cast into prison by Herod, "was sleeping between two soldiers, bound with two chains; and the keepers before the door kept the prison. And, behold, an angel of the Lord came upon him and a light shined in prison." The chains then miraculously fell from Peter's hands, and he followed the angel through the door, moving as if in a vision rather than in an actual escape from his cell.

The story held a special meaning for the great pope who no doubt chose it. Julius II had been the cardinal of the church of St. Peter in Chains in Rome. He was, moreover, an exceptionally active statesman who greatly increased the power of the papacy, so that for him the story referred vividly to the triumph of the descendant of St. Peter over his enemies.

Confronted with an unusual space, a lunette penetrated by a large window, Raphael transformed the disadvantages into a source of strength. He added several soldiers to the traditional representation, and disposed the episodes with such consummate art that, as Wölfflin said, they almost seem to have arranged themselves. He kept the tone of the fresco dark, but over the window (shuttered in the reproduction) he placed the brilliant apparition. Alongside the jambs that recede to the window he painted steps that recede to the prison. The walls of the prison, the exceptional thickness of which magnifies the miracle of escape, rise above and of course "behind" the jambs. The recession into the painted space is very rapid at the left, where soldiers on the steps move with an excitement they did not yet manifest in the drawing of 1511. Raphael had here learned from Michelangelo's revelations on the Sistine ceiling how to heighten the drama of a miraculous event. At the right, where the liberated Saint moves as if in a dream, the soldiers quietly continue to sleep.

As a night scene, Raphael's fresco belongs in the tradition of such paintings as Piero della Francesca's *Dream of Constantine* (page 144). Though in that work there is only one source of light Raphael's more complex composition has four. The brightest light, at the center, becomes almost blinding when seen through the superb device of the contrasting, dark bars. The disturbance at the left, with figures leaning in and out, is enhanced by a dual source of light, a torch nearby and the moon shining in an agitated sky. The angel again lights up the darkness at the right, illuminating the soldiers indirectly by reflection from the unseen face of the wall that recedes between the steps and the window. Everywhere Raphael renders with imagination and joy the flow of light from its sources. His orchestration is magnificent, and it has rarely if ever been equaled.

RAPHAEL, 1513, GALATEA

Rome, Villa Farnesina, Sala di Galatea

While still working on the religious cycle in the room of the *Liberation of St. Peter* Raphael painted a mythological subject in the new Roman villa of the great banker Agostino Chigi. Galatea, a sea nymph who loved Acis, was wooed by Polyphemus. Though Polyphemus was a monster, he courted Galatea with a beautiful song. When she rejected him he hurled a rock at Acis and killed him.

In the Sala di Galatea at the Farnesina Polyphemus, painted by Sebastiano del Piombo in 1511, sits on a cliff, facing the sea and the nymph. Then Raphael represented her nearby as she checks her speeding craft and turns to look at the giant. The painter was familiar with descriptions by ancient and Renaissance writers, but he followed none of them closely. Two flying *putti* aim arrows at Galatea, a third at a Nereid already in the embrace of a sea god. Perhaps the additional arrows held in reserve by a *putto* suggest Galatea's great resistance to Polyphemus. A *putto* astride the water abets those above by tugging at the mouth of a dolphin to slow him down. Two Tritons, one of them on a magnificent sea horse, sound conches to swell the giant's song.

Raphael has not painted one of the climactic moments of the myth. His fresco is rather a celebration of life lived close to nature or, at a deeper level, a eulogy of the harmony of natural forces personified by the gods of the sea. For centuries the harmonious rhythms of his composition and the counterpoint of its spiral movements have delighted painters, critics, and the entire cultivated world—despite, it should be said, some discoloration and retouching of the surface.

A year after painting the fresco Raphael referred to *Galatea* in a famous letter. "In order to paint a beautiful woman I should have to see many beautiful women. . . . but since they are scarce I make use of a certain idea that comes to mind. Whether it has any artistic value I cannot say; I strive just to have it." These direct and simple sentences, inspired by an ancient prototype, express a conviction about the relationship between nature and created beauty in what we have come to call classical art.

The literature on the *Galatea* is vast but two observations, so far as I can see, remain to be made. The painter has put the nymph in Venus' shell, and he has attached to it a paddle wheel—an odd and rather absurd intrusion of a technological interest in this great paradigm of the pagan spirit. Though this concept of propulsion was known since antiquity it was widely diffused only by the publication of Valturio's *De re militari* in 1472. The subject of the ceiling of the Sala di Galatea is very personal; it illustrates the horoscope of the donor, Agostino Chigi. He was perhaps especially interested in Galatea because she personified the foam of the sea, and much of his great fortune came from a monopoly on salt partly extracted from brine.

ANDREA DEL SARTO, 1523, FEAST OF HEROD

Florence, Chiostro allo Scalzo

★

When Raphael and Michelangelo left Florence to work in the Vatican two major painters remained in the city, Fra Bartolommeo (page 184) and Andrea del Sarto. In about 1510 Sarto undertook an important and challenging commission, a series of frescoes for all four walls of the cloister of one of those numerous brotherhoods that served religious, charitable, and social purposes in Italian cities at the time. The walls were to contain the story of John the Baptist, patron of the brotherhood, and four Virtues simulating statues in niches. These Virtues probably suggested the use of monochrome (see Giotto's similar Virtues and Vices, page 43), and the choice was perhaps influenced also by a wish to maintain a close resemblance between the frescoes and the recently completed architecture of the cloister.

Sarto set the scenes in a fictive architecture, the lower part of which has been severely damaged. The figures themselves assume an architectural function, indexing the space and, especially in the *Baptist Preaching* on a following plate, serving as surrogate columns. The *Feast of Herod*, moreover, is the last fresco on one wall, and the imposing "thinker" serves at least as much as the pilaster to block further movement toward the right. At the same time his left arm and tilted head turn our attention from the corner back into the space.

The undisturbed meditation of this man at the very moment when Salome appears bearing the head of the Baptist on a charger is striking and mysterious. Herod, who ordered the decapitation, and Herodias, who plotted the events, respond instantly to the sight, and it affects equally the servants. Their movements of surprise and horror are, however, governed by a principle of rhythmical flow and balance that denies them part of their immediacy and individuality. Even a shocking revelation provides an occasion for strong but poised and graceful gyrations. Disturbance is subsumed in a rich, eurhythmic order.

Sarto attained this kind of composition in the latter part of his career, partly through study of the works of Raphael, Michelangelo, and other artists of the High Renaissance. The *Feast of Herod* is one of the latest scenes in the Scalzo, which were executed over a period of almost fifteen years. The more massive figures swing out into a deeper space. The intervals between them are greater, and the painter has struck a new balance between solid forms and voids. He has retained, at the same time, his soft textures and suffused light.

All the frescoes, in precarious state, were detached in the period 1963–1968, and nine sections formed part of the exhibition.

ANDREA DEL SARTO, 1517, BAPTISM OF THE PEOPLE

Florence, Chiostro allo Scalzo

★

This fresco and the one reproduced opposite meet in the corner of adjoining walls, and Sarto has made them match in certain respects. The similar knolls are side by side. In the *Baptist Preaching* Christ, of whose coming John speaks, appears on the hill, and at a similar place in the *Baptism of the People* John addresses the Pharisees. The two figures in the corner, back to back, correspond; they anticipate in their rotation and their function the "thinker" in the *Feast of Herod*, who also stands near a corner.

This fresco, relatively well preserved, shows that even in monochrome Sarto's brush can achieve richness of texture and, one is tempted to say also, of color. In the group of heads at the left the difference of tone between the bearded man and the others is due to Sarto's miscalculation of the appearance of his color after drying.

ANDREA DEL SARTO, 1515, THE BAPTIST PREACHING

Florence, Chiostro allo Scalzo

★

This scene, on a wall adjacent to the *Baptism of the People* reproduced opposite, is exceptionally simple and symmetrical, and these qualities as well as its repeated verticals show that the painter wished to relate it closely to the columns and space of the small cloister. Sarto could more readily accomplish this kind of equivalence in his earlier work, and this is indeed one of the first frescoes he painted in the series. The figures are more columnar than in the later paintings, without that movement and countermovement—or contrapposto— that characterizes the fully developed High Renaissance style. Although the limbs of the figures do not, as later, extend out into the space the Baptist rotates gracefully on his axis as he addresses an unseen audience behind and beyond the pilaster.

PONTORMO, *ca.* 1514, MADONNA AND SAINTS

Florence, Santissima Annunziata, Chapel of the Academy of Artists

★

Pontormo was Andrea del Sarto's most gifted pupil, and this is his first monumental work, painted just when he had become an independent master. His imagination, still guided by Sarto's example, envisaged a soft, suffused light falling on silky textures. These he enriched with purple and orange-red colors, and rich yellows shaded in warm brown or a beautiful cool violet. From Sarto too came the grandiloquent posture of St. Lucy as she holds aloft her martyred eyes, compelling us to gaze upon them.

Equally insistent is St. Michael; he brandishes his scales near the Virgin and attracts her attention to him. The Child withdraws, in a truly Michelangelesque leap, from the old saint who leans close to him, and the movement generated in this confrontation is carried on by the saint who throws her head back and peers upward, in the direction of God the Father who originally appeared in a lunette above the fresco.

Close as he is to Sarto, Pontormo reveals his own very different taste in the compactness and even compression of the composition and the degree to which one figure impinges upon another. He already preferred an art of higher emotional pitch, and this preference is manifest in the interrupted rhythms and contrasting movements of his design. Pontormo avoids establishing any area of culmination or relative repose, especially at the center where we should expect to find it.

Pontormo painted the fresco for the church of S. Ruffillo, and when that was demolished in 1823 the fresco (without the lunette) was moved, on the entire section of the wall that supported it, to the Chapel of the Academy (see page 214). Seriously threatened by the floodwaters of 1966, it was detached in 1967, disclosing a *sinopia* by an earlier, Filippinesque painter. The *sinopia* represents the Madonna enthroned and at least two of the four saints in the fresco, the Archangel and St. Lucy (who also has the same position). The third saint could be the same as the one with upturned head in the fresco, and the fourth saint just to the right of the Madonna (his halo only faintly visible) is an old man similar to the man in this place in the fresco. The *sinopia* labels him Alexius, and since this rather uncommon saint wrote his life on parchment the kneeling saint might well be he rather than Zacharias, as he has always been called. The unusual tablet or perhaps flat book he holds would then refer to the written life, which was in his hands when he died. This tentative identification is supported by the fact that Alexius was a patron of pilgrims and S. Ruffillo a church for them.

The modern additions to the bottom of the fresco and the repaint, especially in the Madonna, about which writers on Pontormo rightly complained, were all removed in 1967.

PONTORMO, *ca.* 1527, ANNUNCIATION

Florence, Santa Felicità, Capponi Chapel

★

When Ludovico Capponi asked Pontormo to embellish the little chapel in the church of Santa Felicità he had acquired in 1525, it was decided to devote the window-wall opposite the entrance to the Annunciation—to which, indeed, the chapel was dedicated. The choice of this place for the Annunciation conformed to a tradition we have encountered as early as the Lorenzettian fresco at Montesiepi (page 80). The reasons for this preference were both religious and artistic: the importance of the moment of Incarnation, and the suitability of two figures, related and yet in certain respects separated, for the spaces at the sides of the window.

Pontormo, again following some of his predecessors, carried the architecture of the chapel into his fresco, imitating to a degree its refined Brunelleschian forms in the molding he painted around the window and in the arch and capitals with which he articulated the upper reaches of his very high but quite narrow spaces. The arch helps, also, to hold the figures together. Pontormo related his painting to the chapel still further by identifying the source of light for the painting with the actual light coming from the window above (the lower part of the space between the two figures was filled by a monument). Because of these various relationships between the painting and the building the detached fresco, like others of its kind, looks incomplete and somewhat aimless in a museum—at least for those who cannot reconstruct in imagination its setting. We must however admit, in this case as in others, that the original lighting in the chapel left something to be desired. The glare of the window smothered Pontormo's superb painted light and delicate range of colors.

Partly for this reason the exhibition of the fresco, skillfully detached in 1967, has been greeted with the greatest delight. It appeared not only in a good light but also freed of the usual dirt and repaint. The angel in particular had in modern times received a rubbery knee, and his hair and wings had been weakly "strengthened." Cleaning, to be sure, revealed gaps and losses, but it restored to us the glorious original colors in what is beyond doubt one of Pontormo's masterpieces.

The figures in this fresco are based on accumulated Florentine knowledge of the structure and functioning of the human body, but especially in the *Annunciation* Pontormo employed this knowledge for purposes very different from those of most of the painters who contributed to it, such as his teacher Sarto. Pontormo was not concerned with the ponderous, willful actors depicted by many major Florentine artists but, like Botticelli and Filippino, with figures that convey subtle feelings. He adopted the motive of the soaring angel, first introduced, significantly, in Sienese painting. Gabriel flies so rapidly that his orange mantle is swept out by the breeze and he holds fast to the ends of it. The bellying mantle becomes, indeed,

a sail that holds the undeniably weighty form aloft. The inward tilt of the head lightens the figure and balances the disposition of both arms on the nearer side.

The tall Virgin, peering timidly toward the angel, has begun to turn away from him. She clutches her mantle and reaches with her foot for a higher step, in preparation, it seems, for departure. She leans uncertainly and she seems to wilt as her violet scarf falls limply down her body. The color of this scarf is an extraordinary invention, violet in shade and emerald green in light. The shift on the Virgin's head from one of these colors to the other amplifies eloquently her fleeting feelings of surprise and fear. The dark, searching eyes in the pallid face are haunting.

Vasari said the two figures in this painting were so twisted and troubled that one recognizes once again "the bizarre extravagance of that brain," which is never satisfied with anything. Pontormo, he said, excluded everyone, even the patron, from the chapel during the period of execution so that he could carry out the work in his own way. The fresco was finally unveiled, and admired by all Florence.

This account tells us what we had strongly suspected from looking at the work: it was intensely felt, and the painter was aware of a special personal relation to it. Perhaps his isolation helped him maintain the freshness of his vision and the exquisite, vibrant character of the result. The anxiety of the Virgin derogated by Vasari is not, however, very exceptional in the depiction of this event. The astonishing *Annunciation* at Montesiepi (page 81) assures us of that.

PVBLIVS·
MVTIVS·
TRIBVNVS·

DOMENICO BECCAFUMI, 1529–1535, A ROMAN TRIBUNE
CREMATES HIS FELLOWS

Siena, Palazzo Pubblico, Sala del Concistoro

This is a detail of one scene in the last cycle of frescoes painted in the town hall of Siena. It is also the last cycle commissioned by the Republic of this city, which was finally destroyed by the Emperor after a bitter struggle that ended in 1555. The Sienese had in fact regained their freedom only in 1524, after a period of subjection to a tyrant. In that year the *Libertini*, partisans of independence, won power in the city, and with wide popular support they defeated an army of the Medici pope who wished to crush them.

It was in the aftermath of this great victory that the *Libertini* decided to embellish their council hall with frescoes celebrating Justice and the defenders of liberty in Republican Rome. Beccafumi painted figures of Justice, Concord, and *Amor Patriae* on the ceiling, and on the wall or arch that curves into it appear scenes of ancient protectors of freedom. The painter took his episodes from the famous historical compilation written in early Imperial Rome by Valerius Maximus. One of this author's exemplifications of firmness and determination is the action of Publius Mutius, one of the ten Tribunes, political protectors and leaders of the people. When Publius came to believe that his nine colleagues threatened the people's freedom he had them burned alive.

The detail reproduced shows the Tribune directing this cremation, which is enacted in the background. The executioners throw faggots on the roaring fire, which will shortly be fed also by the boy and his dog, the latter carrying a couple of sticks in its mouth. The presence of children at tragic events, particularly at the Passion of Christ, is especially common in early Sienese painting, but the conceit of the dog suggests a certain levity or scepticism on the part of the painter. No one can fail to recognize, however, that he has demonstrated vividly what he was expected to prove: the unwavering determination of Publius Mutius and the extreme measures he was willing to take in the name of liberty.

The subject was in a sense very suitable to Beccafumi. The creator of peculiarly liquid and vaporous forms, he was a very effective painter of fires. This one, pallid as usual, casts a rosy glow on the nearer arch and the ground beneath it. The hellish zone is set off by the cool colors in the foreground. The earth is pale green and the Tribune a beautiful green, blue, and violet.

Beccafumi inserted the stories of Roman heroes as well as the allegorical figures in an illusionistic framework of the kind that had been developed for ceilings in Italian painting of the sixteenth century. Here of course both the tablet bearing the Tribune's name and the shadow it casts are part of the fresco.

CORREGGIO, *ca.* 1518–1522, CHRIST AND THE APOSTLES

Parma, San Giovanni Evangelista, Cupola

Whereas Beccafumi and earlier painters had opened spaces, more or less deep, within painted frames that provided a skeletal structure for a ceiling (page 206), Correggio, undertaking a cupola, introduced a different scheme. The cupola itself, to begin with, lacks the usual lantern at the top that provides light—a change during construction probably proposed by the painter himself. The only natural light is provided by small round windows in the low drum of the dome, and where the lantern would normally be Correggio has painted a luminous glory, at the center of which is the hovering figure of Christ. Christ is surrounded by a host of angels, who grow regularly smaller in proportion to their greater distance from the viewer. Nearer us, and therefore slightly larger in size, are eleven apostles, immersed in a bank of clouds. Following the new Roman manner, the apostles are largely nude. Each reclines in a different way, and Peter, his keys glistening in the light, points toward Christ.

John the Evangelist, patron of the church, does not appear in the clouds but below, on the mound of Patmos; in the reproduction he is visible upside down at the upper edge of the gold cornice. It is in fact his vision that is represented. In each of the pendentives of the dome an evangelist and a Church Father sit on clouds, supported by atlas-like *putti*. In the lower left John discourses with St. Augustine, and at the right Matthew turns away from his book to see what St. Jerome is writing. Even the arches provide fields, however narrow, for figures. There Correggio painted Old Testament worthies, rendering them in sepia to maintain the warmth of color and to suggest a resemblance to bronze.

By painting away the entire surface of the cupola Correggio moved beyond one of his principal models, the ceiling by Mantegna in nearby Mantua (page 163). His field was, furthermore, much larger and higher: an ellipse about 30 by 27 feet, and the top of the cupola about 100 feet above the ground. To create an imposing effect at a distance Correggio adopted, and indeed even increased, the size of the largest figures in Michelangelo's ceiling (page 189). He made his hovering Christ 13 feet high. Though this figure and all the others are foreshortened, Correggio avoided the more startling consequences of a low point of sight that delighted Mantegna. Developing a religious theme, he took advantage instead of the curving cupola and pendentives to tilt most of the figures toward the beholder. He had, nevertheless, to face new problems, especially in the instance of Christ, and one can well believe that to meet them he studied small suspended models in his studio.

Correggio's cupola in S. Giovanni was a landmark in the history of painting, foreshadowing the illusionistic ceilings of the Roman Baroque. The cupola of S. Giovanni was in poor state and quite indistinct until the cleaning finished in 1962, which recovered not only the original fresco surfaces but also some of Correggio's retouching *a secco*.

208

Rome, Vatican, Sistine Chapel

On the wall above the altar of the Sistine Chapel Michelangelo fashioned the most awesome spectacle our civilization has conceived in art. He adopted the tiered composition and the groups of Blessed and Damned employed for this subject by his predecessors, such as Giotto (page 43), but he set the entire throng in sudden and often violent motion. At the center Christ, herculean though much smaller than the gigantic Jonah in the spandrel above, produces a maelstrom by raising his arm in condemnation. Though the usual figures, including the Virgin, gather around him his action fills them with fear. The rise of the Blessed at the left, though tortuous, conveys hope, but the dominant effect of this twisting, plunging mass of bodies is terror and doom. As a final touch, near the center of the fresco the painter has transformed the flayed skin of St. Bartholomew into a nightmarish self-portrait.

The fresco, forty feet high, is far too large for the page of a book, but its mediocre condition and its relation to the windows make it difficult to see well in the chapel. It has been retouched repeatedly, first during the Counter-Reformation when the nude figures in it were given loincloths.

AGNOLO BRONZINO, *ca.* 1543, THE MIRACULOUS
SPRING OF MOSES Detail

Florence, Palazzo Vecchio, Cappella dell'Eleanora

In this fresco the Israelites, having crossed the Red Sea, drink from a spring miraculously produced by Moses, who, as one can barely see in the reproduction, has struck his staff against a rock. The fresco, which continues upward into a lunette, is immediately to the left of a window, so that its position corresponds exactly to that of the awakened guards in Raphael's *Liberation of St. Peter* (page 192). Whereas Raphael had disposed his figures in a space that extends back parallel to the jamb of the window Bronzino crowds his close to the picture plane, weaving them into a pattern of great density and richness. The figures rise one above the other, evenly and clearly lighted, so that they present to us in undiminished beauty every strand of silken hair and the exquisite gradations of tone in every turning plane. The flesh is so smooth it resembles polished marble, even when, as in the back of the drinking man, it is rippled—superbly rippled—by muscles.

Ornaments and drinking bowls are wrought with the refinement of a goldsmith. Bronzino puts everything there for us to see; there is no twilight in his world. Even the face of the youth turned away from the light is visible in beautiful transparent shade. The painter permits no shadows in which elusive but nonetheless real feelings might lurk. True, men and women drink eagerly, a child cries for water, and the thirst of the old man in blue is pathetic—but clearly and single-mindedly pathetic. Otherwise the wanderers in the desert are remarkably elegant, composed and cool.

These are rather constant qualities of Bronzino's figures, regardless of their context. His greater concern with form than with subject associates him with the style we call Mannerism. Though his art has its obvious limits he shows himself here to be a superb painter. His rendering of the transparent water or of the turning, twisting forms along the left margin proves the range of his mastery. He concentrated the warm colors along a central axis while placing the light and mostly cool colors near the waterfall. This pattern is complicated and enriched by shifts in color from light to dark: from green to purple, pale rose to blue, or pale pink to violet.

The frescoes in the chapel were commissioned by Cosimo de' Medici, who became Duke of Florence in 1537, after a tumultuous period in the history of the city. In 1539 he married Eleanora of Toledo, and when the couple then moved into the Palazzo Vecchio numerous enterprises were undertaken. This fresco and the one on the opposite side of the window, representing the Fall of Manna, appear under a large painted chalice. They clearly refer, then, to the Eucharist. Is it possible that they refer also to the benefits that the new and powerful Duke promised to bring to a weary people, and that Cosimo, like some earlier leaders, thought of himself as a new Moses?

ALESSANDRO ALLORI, 1571, TRINITY

Florence, Santissima Annunziata, Chapel of the Academy of Artists

★

The fresco represents the Trinity in the form it acquired in the late Middle Ages, Christ appearing as the pathetic Man of Sorrows. The Florentine Accademia del Disegno, founded in 1562 by forty-eight artists, commissioned the painting for the wall above the altar of their newly acquired chapel in the monastery of the Servites. Since 1349 Florentine artists had been united in a fraternity under the patronage of St. Luke, supposed author of a portrait of the Virgin. Nothing documents more strikingly the subsequent transformation of the painter from craftsman to learned artist than the replacement of the old brotherhood by an academy. The new society proposed to teach painters, sculptors and architects geometry and anatomy as well as technique. The emblem of the old fraternity, Luke's winged ox, was abandoned for a new one: three linked crowns and the motto "They [the arts] raise our intellect from earth to heaven." The Academy of the three arts, symbolized by the crowns, chose the Trinity as chief patron instead of St. Luke. In addition to Allori's fresco, there were two others, one by Vasari showing St. Luke painting the Virgin, another representing Solomon as builder of the Temple. The sculptors thus lacked a fresco of their own; they were represented by one member of the Trinity and by the cycle of statues in the chapel.

By the nineteenth century the intellectual aspirations of the founders of the Academy had been largely forgotten, and the altar of the chapel was moved from the *Trinity* to the fresco of the old patron, St. Luke. Ironically the Chapel of the Academy is now called the Chapel of St. Luke.

The fresco was originally assigned, in 1567, to Bronzino (page 212) and his pupil Allori. No payments were made, however, until 1571, the date inscribed on the left parapet of the fresco, and then the records all refer to lime and sand employed by Allori alone for the *intonaco*. These payments extend over a period of eight days, and the patches of *intonaco* in the fresco indicate execution in seven days.

Despite the documents the *Trinity* was regarded as the last work of Bronzino because the pedestal at the right bears his initials, AN. BR. When the fresco, like the one by Pontormo transported to the Chapel in 1823 (page 201), was damaged by the recent flood and detached in 1967, cleaning of its surface disclosed traces of a portrait bust under Bronzino's initials, and a similar one in the left pedestal under Pontormo's initials. Pontormo was buried in the Chapel in 1562, Bronzino in 1572, and after this second burial portraits of the two illustrious academicians, together with their initials, were added to the *Trinity*. They were added, however, *a secco*, and hence all but their shadow is gone. Even that was discovered only because of a calamity!

TITIAN, 1511, A TREE   Detail of Miracle of St. Anthony

Padua, Scuola del Santo

This is the upper left corner of a fresco representing St. Anthony of Padua healing a woman injured by a jealous husband. The fresco, together with two others in the room painted in the same year, is the earliest documented work by Titian. He was then about twenty-three years old. This small detail is more than enough to demonstrate that at this age he was already a supreme master.

Very few if any painters in history could match this quick, sure evocation of two hilltops, one dark, the other glowing in sunlight. One is covered with dry grasses, the other supports green plants and trees with glistening trunks. The sparse leaves move before a yellow and blue-gray sky. Titian's vision somehow gives every form a meaningful relation to every other form with regard to shape and texture as well as color and light. The painter's love of nature and the poetry of his response to it are enchanting.

Fresco was not Titian's principal technique. He practiced it only occasionally, and what he produced has either been destroyed or badly damaged. His three early frescoes in Padua have suffered for centuries from decay and repainting. In 1969 an Italian national commission, seeking methods to preserve what remains and wishing if possible to recover Titian's original surface, invited the outstanding specialist Leonetto Tintori to clean a corner of one of the frescoes. The breathtaking result is here reproduced.

PAOLO VERONESE, 1561–1562, SALONE

Asolo (Maser), Villa Barbaro

To stand in the villa at Maser is a rare and elevating experience. The photographer has set his camera near the center of the cruciform room that constitutes the main hall or *salone* of the building. The camera, facing two of the eight walls of the *salone*, has caught the few handsome forms with which the architect Palladio articulated these walls: a white plaster frieze as well as a pediment and some moldings around a rectangle that imply a door. The door itself and the rest of the architecture issued from the brush of the painter Paolo Veronese. He conjured up, too, the little girl peeking through the partly opened leaves of the painted door and the players of music in niches. These figures, who cast shadows on the wall, seem to extend out of the fictive space into the actual—the violin appears to be as far in front of the wall as the actual pediment. Inasmuch as they bear, furthermore, natural colors and textures they have the qualities both of women and of statues. On the other hand the satyr's head over the door, the reclining men just below it, and the bronze "Victories" in the spandrels over the arch are unequivocally simulated statues or reliefs.

If the camera were rotated more toward the left it would catch a part of the fertile plain lying below the villa, framed by a window in the end wall. Veronese has himself opened the adjoining wall, as we see, onto a balcony and a view of a rugged terrain leading to a large ruined arch. The painter introduced ruins in this and several other landscapes as symbols of the noble culture of the past by which his own was greatly enriched.

The painter gave the walls of the villa, and often also the vaults and ceilings, not merely a complete but a consistent illusionism. This sustained metaphor distinguishes the painting of Maser from almost everything that preceded it. No wonder it surprises and enchants everyone who enters the building.

The imagination of Veronese was nurtured by a long tradition that reaches back, as we have seen, through Correggio (page 209) to Mantegna (page 159), Giotto (page 43), and ancient Rome (page 26). Before painting Maser, Veronese might indeed have seen fragments of ancient painting in, for instance, the Colosseum or the recently discovered Golden House of Nero on the Esquiline Hill in Rome.

Of course it is not only the breathtaking illusionism of Veronese's frescoes that makes them so memorable, nor the wit and fantasy of his inventions. Within the magnificent, strict proportions of Palladio's villa he shaped his own gayer and more sensuous structures. Into the areas of white he inserted pale colors, violet, yellow-brown, and green. The woman holding violin and bow, relaxed before or after playing, turns slowly and quietly as she guides the visitor, so to speak, from one part of the room to another.

PAOLO VERONESE AND ASSISTANT, 1561–1562,
SALA DELLA LUCERNA

Asolo (Maser), Villa Barbaro

The reproduction shows a narrow wall, up to the real frieze, of one of the smaller rooms called the *Lucerna* because of the oil-lamp that hangs from the ceiling before a Holy Family that is painted above the frieze. The opposite wall contains a window that looks onto the pool of the nymphaeum, and Veronese has provided an equivalent window with a marine view. In the fictive architecture he included niches with statues that resemble the actual statues provided for many rooms of the villa by the Venetian sculptor Alessandro Vittoria. For clusters of buildings in several landscapes Veronese drew from slightly earlier engravings by Cock and Battista Pittoni. He seems to have used a print by the latter for part of the landscape reproduced, which was executed by an assistant.

Veronese's program for the villa was inspired not only by preceding Renaissance schemes of decoration and by the few remains of ancient murals that he could have known but also by descriptions of the paintings in Roman villas in the writings of Vitruvius and Pliny. Pliny referred to murals in country houses that depicted gardens, woods, hills, rivers and coasts, and Vitruvius spoke of "harbors, headlands, shores, rivers, springs, straits, temples, groves, hills, cattle, shepherds." In his treatise on architecture of about 1450, Alberti, familiar with these texts, asserted that the decoration of country villas, as distinct from town houses, should be gay and fanciful. Daniele Barbaro, one of the brothers for whom the villa had been built and decorated, was a scholar, a student of mathematics, of philosophy, and of architecture, and indeed just before the building of Maser he had himself published an annotated translation of Vitruvius' treatise.

The glories of Maser are thus the result of a conjunction of a very gifted, scholarly patron, a great architect, a painter scarcely less great, and a very good sculptor. This combination is rare in history, even during the Italian Renaissance.

PAOLO VERONESE, 1561–1562, LANDSCAPE   Detail

Asolo (Maser), Villa Barbaro, Sala dell'Olimpo

This is a detail of one of the most beautiful landscapes in the villa, surely painted by Veronese himself. On a plain near a river a shepherd tends his sheep, their white wool bright against the rich green grass. Two large barges move on the river; one of them carries enormous logs, greater in diameter than the large trunk cut from the stump in the foreground. Beyond the river rises a green hill and then cold gray mountains, reminiscent of the Dolomites, which lie not far to the north of the wall on which this imaginary landscape appears.

The world around the river is shaped and controlled by man, but he cannot contend with the mountains. Veronese has given them a titanic force by the seemingly simple expedient of drawing his brush laden with varying shades of gray across the white ground. The quite visible streaks of the bristles animate the masses, most of the lower ones surging sideways, the higher ones leaping upward like flames. Rays of sunlight that dramatically break through the clouds reduce the severity of this awesome prospect.

The marvelous paintings of the Villa Maser have not always been appreciated or even respected. For a long time the building was abandoned, and then in the nineteenth century the murals were "restored," a process that too often signified repainting. Their survival is due to the fact that they were painted in the fresco technique. In recent years, under the care of the present enlightened owners, they have been expertly cleaned and maintained.

ANNIBALE CARRACCI AND ASSISTANTS, 1597–1600, CEILING

Rome, Palazzo Farnese, Galleria

The Galleria, designed to exhibit ancient statues, measures only about 66 by 20 feet, but it is covered by the gayest and perhaps the most sumptuous ceiling in that city of great ceilings, Rome. It delights the eye by its bright color, robust forms, and rhythmical unity while it piques the understanding by its continually unfolding illusions. Simulated stone herms and atlantes carry into the vault the lines of the pilasters below and seem to bear the weight of the three paintings set into the ridge of the vault. The largest of these pictures, the *Triumph of Bacchus and Ariadne,* has a white frame whereas the picture nearer us of Mercury plunging down to Paris with the golden apple and the corresponding picture at the far end of the vault are framed in gold. The three other pictures framed in gold—Aurora and Cephalus at the left, a corresponding scene at the right, and Polyphemus on the far wall— have a different kind of reality. They are clearly easel paintings placed "temporarily" on the cornice against the wall; they overlap both its ornamentation and the bronze medallions set into it. A fourth category of pictures, including Diana with Endymion at the right, has white stone or stucco frames, but unlike those in the *Triumph of Bacchus and Ariadne* they are set into the wall and they are overlapped by the simulated herms and atlantes.

The multilayered wall is lacking in the corners, and there we catch a glimpse of a balustrade surmounted by *putti* before a blue sky. The picture nearest these deep views has itself an exceptional depth; Polyphemus swings back before hurling a boulder at Galatea's fleeing lover, Acis. In the distance beyond Acis runs the terrified nymph herself. Diminution in space has reduced her to the size of the *putti*. The arms of the simulated statues at the sides of the picture echo the movement of Polyphemus, and the rage of the monster seems related to the agitated posture of the nude man seated to the right of him.

These are only a few of the countless interrelationships that make the Farnese ceiling one of the greatest paintings of the seventeenth century. Annibale's sophisticated scheme involved overlapping and interpenetration as well as the juxtaposition of complete and incomplete forms. By these means he produced the surging movements that give his art, which we call Early Baroque, its dynamic character.

The exuberance of the frescoes is like a revival, at a higher pitch, of Raphael's mythological scenes, such as his *Galatea* (page 195). Annibale's stories, based chiefly on Ovid and selected by learned advisors, recount the loves of the gods. Despite their sensuousness the representations have occasionally been read as allegories of divine love. If, as seems probable, they were painted for the marriage in 1600 of Ranuccio Farnese they celebrate the event in the spirit of an ancient nuptial song or Epithalamium. They demonstrate that mythological beings, like others, have moments of frustration and sorrow as well as of triumph and ecstasy.

PIETRO DA CORTONA, 1637, THE AGE OF GOLD

Florence, Palazzo Pitti, Sala della Stufa

In the spring of 1637 Pietro da Cortona interrupted his work on the vast ceiling in the Palazzo Barberini in Rome to travel north. When the famous painter arrived in Florence on June 28 the young Grand Duke of Tuscany, Ferdinand II, persuaded him to stay and fresco a room in his palace. A month later Pietro wrote to his Roman patron, Cardinal Barberini, that he was working on the *Age of Gold* and an adjoining fresco. In another letter in September the artist said that "the fresco part" of the two paintings was finished, and that he needed only to complete them (*a secco*, of course).

When the Grand Duke persuaded Pietro da Cortona to fresco a room he, like Ranuccio Farnese (page 224), had a wedding in mind; he was about to celebrate his marriage to Vittoria della Rovere. Instead of selecting a subject from the Old Testament to allude to his significance for Florence, as his predecessor Cosimo I seems, in our opinion, to have done (page 212), he accepted the proposal of a councillor to represent Ovid's Four Ages of Man. The Age of Gold, according to the *Metamorphoses*, was succeeded by the Age of Silver (also painted by Cortona in July), the Age of Bronze, and finally the Age of Iron, the ultimate stage in the steady decline.

Here is part of Ovid's description of the earthly paradise of the Age of Gold: "The earth herself, without compulsion, untouched by hoe or plowshare, of herself gave all things needful. And men, content with food which came with no one's seeking, gathered the arbute fruit, strawberries from the mountainsides, cornel-cherries, berries hanging thick upon the prickly bramble, and acorns fallen from the spreading tree of Jove. Then spring was everlasting, and gentle zephyrs with warm breath played with the flowers that sprang unplanted."

Now the tree of Jove was also the tree of the young bride's family, the Rovere. In the fresco a man tugs on a branch of the oak that is laden with acorns, and a *putto* carries branches of this tree to the nude youth at the left, obviously a metaphor for the Duke. A young girl, who alludes to the bride, crowns him with the laurel of *vittoria* (victory). A nymph brandishes another wreath of laurel, and above fly a pair of turtle doves, symbols of marital fidelity. All the animals, including the deer in the distance, live fearlessly with man, and the lion, symbol of Florence (see page 175), reclines peacefully under a bundle of oak leaves. The only product of "civilized" techniques is the gold dish in the right foreground. The Age of Gold, Ovid's first and highest, will return to Florence under the rule of Ferdinand II and Vittoria.

Pietro da Cortona has evoked a bounteous nature warmed by a bright sun, entirely hospitable to a carefree gathering. The general happiness is contagious, whatever reservations we may have about the promise of the Medici. The light, limpid colors, the fluid forms, and the rippling movements all contribute to the gaiety. This is one of the most attractive of Italian Baroque paintings.

GIOVANNI BATTISTA TIEPOLO, 1725–1728, THE ANGEL RESCUES HAGAR AND ISHMAEL

SACRIFICE OF ISAAC (overleaf)

Udine, Arcivescovado, Galleria

Painting on ceilings is not, as we have seen, always the same thing as painting on walls, and different periods approached it in different ways. The insubstantial figures of the Middle Ages could be transferred from wall to ceiling with little if any change (page 31), but a problem was created by the distribution overhead of the weighty figures of Giotto's era, which were basically conceived in relation to gravitational pull. The introduction of deep space and focus perspective presented further challenges, together with new opportunities. We have seen the various solutions of numerous painters, Benozzo Gozzoli (page 157), Mantegna (page 163), Michelangelo (page 189), Correggio (page 209), and Annibale Carracci (page 225). Where the figures were sculptural, or even simulated stone, a strong architectural structure gave them the requisite support. Masters such as Pontormo (page 203) and Correggio contrived to make the massive Renaissance figures fly.

Heir to this magnificent tradition, the young Tiepolo painted a series of marvelous frescoes in what was then the Patriarchate at Udine. Only about thirty years old, he seems to have been developing his buoyant forms primarily for spaces overhead. They appear to be fashioned of air and color rather than of solid substance. He gave them an enchanting freshness and animation, transforming the pictorial field into a whirlpool of lines, color, and light. The artist retained, however, absolute command of the tempo. Below the pirouetting angel in the *Sacrifice of Isaac*, one of the most glorious floating figures in all art, Tiepolo carefully set the still, earthbound ram.

The scale of the *Sacrifice* is grand, with its arc of clouds and its great heavenly beam, but the story remains simple and touching. Isaac, surprisingly seen from below, engages us with his youthful, innocent countenance. An obedient son, he seems not yet aware of the raised knife or the angel's intervention. The drama is heightened by his close compositional relationship to his father, the two figures crowning a pyramid built of the rarest colors.

The paint is equally magical in the fresco of Hagar, and the story no less freshly conceived and appealing. Again the Lord intervenes at the crucial moment. Ishmael sleeps, his faintness from thirst suggested by a sort of perspective collapse. His remarkably youthful mother,

who has been weeping in her mantle over the empty water barrel, lifts her face to the angel, who tells her of the nearby well. It is not inappropriate that for this life-giving gesture Tiepolo employed the famous life-receiving arm of Michelangelo's Adam. This is one of the countless ways in which the incomparable Italian tradition guided and enriched the painting of Tiepolo, the last brilliant artist of the ceiling and the last great master of a kind of fresco technique.

GLOSSARY

BIBLIOGRAPHIES

INDEX

GLOSSARY

Page numbers in italics refer to illustration pages.

Affresco (in English usage, "fresco"). Painting with pigments dissolved in water on freshly laid plaster. As both plaster and paint dry they become completely integrated. Known as "true" fresco, this technique was most popular from the late thirteenth to the mid-sixteenth centuries. See pages 14–21, *passim.*

Arriccio. The preliminary layer of plaster spread on the masonry. On this layer the *sinopia* is executed. The *arriccio* was left rough so that the final top layer (see *Intonaco*) might more easily adhere. See pages 16, 32, 124, 127.

Cartone (in English usage, "cartoon"). The artist's final drawing on paper or cloth of the main lines of his composition equal in size to the wall area to be painted. The cartoon was laid against the wall over the final freshly laid plaster on which the painting was to be done. Its outlines were incised on the plaster through the heavy paper by pressure from a stylus. The resulting lines guided the artist in painting. This procedure was common in the sixteenth century. See also *Spolvero.* See pages 16, 18, 136, 139, 151, 153.

Giornata. The patch of *intonaco* to be painted in one day. The artist decided in advance the size of the surface he could paint in a day and laid on top of the *arriccio* or rough plaster only the amount of fresh *intonaco* or fine plaster needed for this work. The joinings usually are discernible upon a close examination of the painted surface, and they disclose the order in which the patches were painted because each successive patch slightly overlaps the preceding. See pages 18, 32, 127, 145; *19, 35, 126.*

Intonaco. The final, smooth layer of plaster for the finished painting. It was made from lime and sand and laid in sections, according to the amount of work an artist planned to execute in a day. See pages 16, 18–20, 32, 35, 37, 45, 48, 55, 60, 77, 82, 83, 124, 126, 127, 136, 145, 175, 214; *17, 19, 33.*

Mezzo fresco. Painting on partially dry plaster. The pigment penetrates the plaster less deeply than with the "true" fresco method, and the carbonation is less extensive. *Mezzo fresco* was a popular procedure in the sixteenth and later centuries. See pages *229, 230, 231.*

Pontata. Intonaco spread in wide bands that correspond to successively lower stages of the scaffold. The painter frequently laid some preparatory colors on these large surfaces as they were drying, but he usually spread his final colors after the *intonaco* had dried. This is largely, then, a *secco* technique. See pages 16, 37; *17.*

Secco (literally "dry"). Painting on plaster that has already dried. The colors are mixed with an adhesive or binder. See pages 14–18, 20, 32, 37, 45, 50, 58, 60, 69, 77, 82, 97, 106, 123, 153, 158, 179, 208.

Sinopia. Originally a red ochre named after Sinope, a town on the Black Sea that was well known for its red pigments. In fresco technique the term was used for the final preparatory drawing on the *arriccio,* which was normally executed in red ochre. See pages 16, 18, 32, 34, 56, 80, 83, 84, 88, 106, 121, 151, 153, 200; *34, 57, 61, 81, 83, 90, 108, 120, 150, 154.*

Spolvero (dusting or pouncing). An early method (see *Cartone*) of transferring the artist's drawing onto the *intonaco.* After drawings as large as the frescoes were made on paper, their outlines were pricked, and the paper was cut into pieces the size of each day's work. After the day's patch of *intonaco* was laid, the corresponding drawing was placed over it and "dusted" with a cloth sack filled with charcoal powder, some of which passed through the tiny punctured holes to mark the design on the fresh *intonaco.* This method was most popular in the second half of the fifteenth century. See pages 16, 17, 136, 151, 153.

Stacco. The process of detaching a fresco painting from the wall by removing the pigment and the *intonaco.* Usually an animal glue is applied to the painted surface and then two layers of cloth (calico and canvas) are applied, left to dry, and later stripped off the wall, pulling the fresco with them. It is taken to a laboratory where the excess plaster is scraped away and another cloth is attached to its back. Finally the cloths on the face of the fresco are carefully removed. The fresco is then ready to be mounted on a new support. See pages 16; *17, 110, 111.*

Strappo. The process by which a fresco painting is detached when the plaster on which it is painted has greatly deteriorated. *Strappo* is the process of taking off only the color layer with very small amounts of plaster. It is effected by the use of a glue considerably stronger than that used in the *stacco* technique. The procedure which follows is identical with that in the *stacco* operation. After certain frescoes are removed by means of *strappo* a colored imprint may still be seen on the plaster remaining on the wall. This is evidence of the depth to which the pigment penetrated the plaster. These traces of color are often removed by a second *strappo* operation on the same wall. See pages *53, 57, 59, 129, 155, 184, 196, 198, 199, 201, 203.*

Tempera. The medium added to paint in order to bind the color to the surface to be painted. The binding medium may be made from various substances, but the term refers most often to the addition of egg to pigments. Tempera was commonly used to complete a composition already painted in fresco. Because the pigment and the dry wall surface do not become thoroughly united, as they do in true fresco, mural paintings done in tempera (or *a secco*) tend to deteriorate more rapidly. See pages 15, 18, 20, 46, 48, 50, 66.

BIBLIOGRAPHY FOR FRESCO PAINTING

Listed in Order of Composition

ORIGINAL SOURCES

Vitruvius on Architecture (Loeb Library), London, 1934, II, Book VII, Chapters 3–5. Written during reign of Emperor Augustus (27 B.C.–14 A.D.).

Cennino Cennini, *The Craftsman's Handbook* (translated by D. V. Thompson, Jr.), New Haven, 1933; New York (paperback). Written in early fifteenth century.

Giorgio Vasari, *The Lives of the Painters, Sculptors, and Architects.* 1st ed. 1550; 2nd ed. 1568; several English translations.

Vasari on Technique (translated by L. S. Maclehose), New York, 1960 (paperback).

Andrea Pozzo, *Rules and Examples of Perspective for Painters, Architects, and Others*, London, 1707 (translated from Italian).

MODERN STUDIES

D. V. Thompson, Jr., *The Materials of Medieval Painting*, New Haven, 1936.

R. Oertel, "Wandmalerei und Zeichnung in Italien," in *Mitteilungen des Kunsthistorischen Institutes in Florenz*, V, 1940, pp. 217–314.

U. Procacci, *La tecnica degli antichi affreschi e il loro distacco e restauro*, Florence, 1958.

E. Borsook, *The Mural Painters of Tuscany, from Cimabue to Andrea del Sarto*, London, 1960.

M. Muraro, *Pitture murali nel Veneto*, Venice, 1960.

U. Procacci, *Sinopie e affreschi*, Florence, 1960.

L. Tintori and M. Meiss, *The Painting of the Life of St. Francis in Assisi with Notes on the Arena Chapel*, New York, 1962; 1967 (Norton paperback).

L. Tintori and M. Meiss, "Additional Observations on Italian Mural Technique," *Art Bulletin*, XLVI, 1964, pp. 377–380.

L. Tintori and E. Borsook, *Giotto, The Peruzzi Chapel*, New York, 1965.

A. Chastel, "Peinture murale et peinture sur toile," in *Le grand atelier d'Italie, 1460–1500*, Paris [1965], p. 209 ff.

U. Procacci, Introduction to *The Great Age of Fresco, Giotto to Pontormo* (Catalogue), New York, 1968.

D. C. Winfield, "Middle and Later Byzantine Wall Painting Methods," *Dumbarton Oaks Papers*, XXII, 1968, pp. 63–139.

SELECTED BIBLIOGRAPHY FOR THE
FRESCOES REPRODUCED

A few publications are listed for each fresco. They have been chosen either because they are related in one way or another to my text on the fresco or because they offer the reader recent informed opinion about the fresco and its painter. Most of these publications refer to other studies that discuss the fresco so that they provide an entry into the relevant art-historical literature.

Information of a more general or a more elementary kind is available in numerous handbooks of the history of art or of painting. Since readers will turn to whatever volume is at hand, no purpose would be served by listing them here.

"*Catalogue*" in the following bibliography always refers to:

The Great Age of Fresco, Giotto to Pontormo, New York, The Metropolitan Museum of Art, 1968.

P. 24 Santa Croce
Walter and Elizabeth Paatz, *Die Kirchen von Florenz*, Frankfurt, I, 1940, p. 497ff.; John White, *Art and Architecture in Italy 1250–1400*, Harmondsworth, 1966, p. 8f.

P. 27 Roman, Boscoreale
Phyllis Williams Lehmann, *Roman Wall Painting from Boscoreale in the Metropolitan Museum of Art*, Cambridge, Mass., 1953.

P. 28 Roman, Villa of Livia
Mabel M. Gabriel, *Livia's Garden Room at Prima Porta*, New York, 1955; Michelangelo Cagiano de Azevedo, *Enciclopedia dell'arte antica*, Rome, I, 1958, p. 100f., s. v. *Affresco*.

P. 30 Byzantine, S. Apollinare in Classe
André Grabar, *Byzantine Painting* [Geneva, 1963], p. 73; Mario Mazzotti, *La Basilica di Sant'Apollinare in Classe*, Città del Vaticano, 1954, pp. 101, 168, 178f.

P. 32 Pistoiese Thirteenth Century, Crucifixion
Ugo Procacci, "Romanico pistoiese," in *Atti del I convegno internazionale di studi medioevali di storia e d'arte 1964*, 1966, p. 363; Umberto Baldini, *La Nazione*,

Florence, Feb. 13, 1968; *idem*, in *Catalogue*, p. 50ff., no. 1.

P. 37 Roman, c. 1290, Creation of Eve
Beda Kleinschmidt, *Die Basilika San Francesco in Assisi*, Berlin, 1926, II, p. 63f.; Leonetto Tintori and Millard Meiss, *The Painting of the Life of St. Francis in Assisi with Notes on the Arena Chapel*, New York, 1962, p. 11.

P. 38 Giotto (?), Esau Seeking Isaac's Blessing
Kleinschmidt, *op. cit.*, p. 71; Cesare Gnudi, *Giotto*, Milan, 1958, p. 55f.; Millard Meiss, *Giotto and Assisi*, New York, 1960, p. 11ff.

P. 40 Giotto or a Contemporary, St. Francis
Kleinschmidt, *op. cit.*, p. 108, fig. 73; John White, *Art and Architecture in Italy 1250–1400*, Harmondsworth, 1966, p. 136ff., fig. 73.

P. 42 Giotto, Arena Chapel, Interior
Giotto: The Arena Chapel Frescoes, ed. James H. Stubblebine, New York [1969]. Essays by the editor, R. Offner, M. Alpatoff, D. C. Shorr, U. Schlegel, L. Tintori and M. Meiss.

Pp. 45, 46 Giotto, Expulsion of Joachim; Return of Joachim
Cesare Gnudi, *Giotto*, Milan, 1958, p. 128ff.; Millard Meiss, *Giotto and Assisi*, New York, 1960, p. 6f. (Norton paperback, 1967); Leonetto Tintori and Millard Meiss, *The Painting of the Life of St. Francis in Assisi with Notes on the Arena Chapel*, New York, 1962, p. 160ff.

P. 48 Giotto, Expulsion of the Merchants
Tintori and Meiss, *op. cit.*, p. 169ff., fig. 62; Laurine M. Bongiorno, "The Theme of the Old and the New Law in the Arena Chapel," *Art Bulletin*, L, 1968, pp. 17–19; Ursula Schlegel in *Giotto: The Arena Chapel Frescoes, cit.*, p. 85f.

P. 50 Giotto, Defeat of the Sultan's Priests
Cesare Gnudi, *Giotto*, Milan, 1958, p. 212f.; Millard Meiss, *Giotto and Assisi*, New York, 1960, p. 9, pls. 20–23; John White, *Art and Architecture in Italy 1250–1400*, Harmondsworth, 1966, p. 219ff., pl. 96 B.

P. 52   Giotto Workshop, Head of a Shepherd
Ugo Procacci, "La tavola di Giotto dell'altar maggiore della chiesa della Badia fiorentina," in *Scritti di storia dell'arte in onore di Mario Salmi*, II, 1962, p. 9 ff.; Giovanni Previtali, *Giotto*, Milan, 1967, p. 318; Ugo Procacci, in *Catalogue*, p. 60 ff., no. 4.

P. 55   Taddeo Gaddi, Annunciation to the Shepherds
Robert Oertel, *Early Italian Painting to 1400*, New York, 1968, p. 190.

P. 56   Taddeo Gaddi, Transfiguration
Umberto Baldini, *La Nazione*, Florence, Dec. 6, 1967; *idem*, in *Catalogue*, p. 74, nos. 8, 9.

P. 58   Taddeo Gaddi, Madonna del Parto
Caroline Feudale, "Iconography of the Madonna del Parto," *Marsyas*, VII, 1957, p. 8 ff.; Ugo Procacci, in *Catalogo della mostra di Firenze ai tempi di Dante*, Florence, 1966, p. 102; Paolo Dal Poggetto, in *Catalogue*, p. 72, no. 7.

P. 60   Fogg Master, Head of St. Onophrius
Richard Offner, *Corpus of Florentine Painting*, New York, section III, VI, 1956, pp. ix ff., 65 ff.; Millard Meiss, "Una pittura murale del Maestro della *Pietà Fogg*," *Bollettino d'arte*, LIV, 1966 (appeared 1969), p. 149 ff.; Giuseppe Marchini, "Giovanni di Bonnino," in *Atti del congresso giottesco 1967* (in press); Millard Meiss, in *Catalogue*, p. 90 ff., no. 14.

P. 60   Maso di Banco, Miracle of St. Sylvester
John White, *Art and Architecture in Italy 1250–1400*, Harmondsworth, 1966, p. 269 f.

P. 64   Della Robbia, Tomb
Hannelore Glasser, "The Litigation concerning Luca della Robbia's Federighi Tomb" and Gino Corti, "New Documents," *Mitteilungen des Kunsthistorischen Institutes in Florenz*, XIV, 1969, p. 1 ff.

P. 65   Alesso, Tomb
Giuseppe Marchini, *Il tesoro del duomo di Prato*, Milan, 1963, p. 42; Millard Meiss, "Alesso di Andrea," in *Atti del congresso giottesco 1967* (in press), p. 349 ff.

P. 66   Alesso, Hope
Ugo Procacci, "Quattro Virtù di Alesso di Andrea scoperte nella cappella di S. Jacopo nel duomo di Pistoia," in *Studien zur toskanischen Kunst* (*L. H. Heydenreich Festschrift*), Munich, 1964, p. 244 ff.; Meiss, *op. cit.*, pp. 335–341, 350–351.

P. 69   P. Lorenzetti, Madonna
Ernest De Wald, "Pietro Lorenzetti," *Art Studies*, XCVII, 1929, p. 151 ff.; Cesare Brandi, *Pietro Lorenzetti, affreschi nella basilica di Assisi*, Rome (n. d.), fig. I; Carlo Volpe, *Pietro Lorenzetti ad Assisi*, Milan (n. d.).

P. 70   P. Lorenzetti, Last Supper
De Wald, *op. cit.*, p. 151 f.; Erwin Panofsky, *Renaissance and Renascences in Western Art*, Stockholm, 1960, p. 143 ff., fig. 105.

Pp. 72, 75   Martini, St. Martin Before Emperor Julian; Knighting of St. Martin
Eve Borsook, *The Mural Painters of Tuscany, from Cimabue to Andrea del Sarto*, London, 1960, p. 133 f., pl. 16; John White, *Art and Architecture in Italy 1250–1400*, Harmondsworth, 1966, p. 233 ff.; Ferdinando Bologna, *Gli affreschi di Simone Martini ad Assisi*, Milan (n. d.); Giovanni Paccagnini, *Simone Martini*, Milan (n. d.), p. 70 ff.

P. 77   P. Lorenzetti, St. John
Ernest De Wald, "Pietro Lorenzetti," *Art Studies*, XCVII, 1929, p. 150.

P. 78   A. Lorenzetti, The Good City
George Rowley, *Ambrogio Lorenzetti*, Princeton, 1958, I, p. 112 ff., pl. 157; Enzo Carli, in A. Cairola and E. Carli, *Il Palazzo Pubblico di Siena*, Rome, 1963, p. 119 ff.; John White, *Art and Architecture in Italy 1250–1400*, Harmondsworth, 1966, p. 252 ff.

P. 80   A. Lorenzetti, Annunciation
Millard Meiss, in *Catalogue*, p. 64 ff. nos. 5, 6; Eve Borsook, *Gli affreschi di Montesiepi, con annotazioni tecniche di Leonetto Tintori*, Florence, 1969, p. 27 ff. (on p. 17 an incorrect summary of the attributions proposed in the preceding catalogue entry); Juergen and Anne Markham Schulz, Review of exhibition "The Great Age of Fresco in New York," *Burlington Magazine*, CXI, 1969, p. 51 ff.; Hendrik W. van Os, "Marginal Notes on 'The Great Age of Fresco,'" *Simiolus*, IV, 1969–70 (in press).

P. 84   A. Lorenzetti, Madonna and Saints
George Rowley, *Ambrogio Lorenzetti*, Princeton, 1958, I, p. 64 ff., pls. 82–86.

P. 86   Barna, Crucifixion
Millard Meiss, *Painting in Florence and Siena after the Black Death*, Princeton, 1951, p. 54 ff.; Eve Borsook, *The Mural Painters of Tuscany, from Cimabue to Andrea*

del Sarto, London, 1960, p. 138f., pls. 33, 34; John White, *Art and Architecture in Italy 1250–1400*, Harmondsworth, 1966, p. 361ff.

P. 88 Traini, The Damned
Meiss, *op. cit.*, p. 76, fig. 87; Joseph Polzer, "Aristotle, Mohammed and Nicholas V in Hell," *Art Bulletin*, XLVI, 1964, pp. 457–469; Robert Oertel, *Early Italian Painting to 1400*, New York, 1968, p. 307f.; Millard Meiss, "Alesso di Andrea," in *Atti del congresso giottesco 1967* (in press), p. 341ff.

Pp. 92, 95 Orcagna, The Damned in Hell; The Blind and Halt Appeal to Death
Millard Meiss, *Painting in Florence and Siena after the Black Death*, Princeton, 1951, pp. 14, 74, 83f.; Umberto Baldini, *Mostra di affreschi staccati*, Exhibition Catalogue, Florence, 1958, p. 13ff.; Richard Offner, *Corpus of Florentine Painting*, New York, section IV, I, 1962, p. 43ff.; Paolo Dal Poggetto, in *Catalogue*, p. 78ff., nos. 10, 11; Millard Meiss, "Alesso di Andrea," in *Atti del congresso giottesco 1967* (in press), p. 349.

P. 97 Nardo di Cione, Apostle
Offner, *op. cit.*, section IV, II, 1960, p. 47ff., plate X; Robert Oertel, *Early Italian Painting to 1400*, New York, 1968, p. 242.

P. 98 Giovanni da Milano, Meeting of Joachim and Anna
Millard Meiss, *Painting in Florence and Siena after the Black Death*, Princeton, 1951, p. 25f., pl. 27; Mina Gregori, *Giovanni da Milano alla Cappella Rinuccini*, Milan, 1965; Miklòs Boskovits, *Giovanni da Milano*, Florence, 1966, p. 17ff., pl. 38.

P. 100 Altichiero, Crucifixion
Gian Lorenzo Mellini, *Altichiero e Jacopo Avanzi*, Milan, 1965, p. 57ff.; John White, *Art and Architecture in Italy 1250–1400*, Harmondsworth, 1966, p. 378f., pl. 175.

P. 102 Pistoiese Master, Mary Magdalen
Umberto Baldini, in *Mostra di affreschi staccati*, Exhibition Catalogue, Florence, 1958, p. 22f., no. 25; *idem*, in *Catalogue*, p. 94, no. 15.

P. 102 Starnina, Head of St. Benedict
Raimond van Marle, *The Development of the Italian Schools of Painting*, The Hague, III, 1924, p. 565ff.; Ugo Procacci, "Gherardo Starnina," *Rivista d'arte*, XV, 1933, pp. 151–191, XVII, 1935, pp. 333–384; Paolo Dal Poggetto, in *Catalogue*, p. 102ff.

P. 104 Lorenzo Monaco, Head of a Priest
Osvald Sirén, *Don Lorenzo Monaco*, Strasbourg, 1905, p. 123ff., pl. XLVI; Mirella Levi D'Ancona, "Some New Attributions to Lorenzo Monaco," *Art Bulletin*, XL, 1958, p. 177.

P. 106 Parri Spinelli, Crucifixion
Pierpaolo Donati, "Notizie e appunti su Parri Spinelli," *Antichità viva*, III, 1964, no. 1, p. 23; Luciano Berti, in *Catalogue*, p. 140ff.

P. 107 Masolino, Two Saints
Mario Salmi, *Masaccio*, Milan, 1948, p. 84; Paolo Dal Poggetto and Umberto Baldini, in *Catalogue*, p. 112ff.

Pp. 113, 114 Masaccio, Tribute Money; St. Peter Distributing Money
Herbert von Einem, *Masaccios "Zingroschen,"* Cologne, 1967; Luciano Berti, *Masaccio*, University Park, Pa., 1967, pp. 70ff., 90ff., pl. 46.

Pp. 117, 119 Fra Angelico, Transfiguration; Annunciation
John Pope-Hennessy, *Fra Angelico*, London, 1952, pp. 21f., 183; Mario Salmi, *Il beato Angelico*, Spoleto, 1958, p. 42f.

P. 120 Aranci Master, Miracle of the Raven
Ugo Procacci, *Sinopie e affreschi*, Milan, 1960, pp. 27f., 228f.; Millard Meiss and Luciano Berti, in *Catalogue*, p. 150f., nos. 39, 40.

P. 123 Pisanello, Arms of the Pellegrini Family
George F. Hill, *Pisanello*, London, 1905, p. 91; Bernhard Degenhart, *Antonio Pisanello*, Vienna, 1940, p. 32f.; Maria Fossi Todorow, *I disegni del Pisanello e della sua cerchia*, Florence, 1966, pp. 24, 65.

P. 123 Uccello, Monument of John Hawkwood
John Pope-Hennessy, *The Complete Work of Paolo Uccello*, London, 1950, pp. 7ff., 142; Horst W. Janson, "The Equestrian Monument from Cangrande della Scala to Peter the Great," in *Aspects of the Renaissance*, Austin, 1967, p. 79ff.; Bernhard Degenhart and Annegrit Schmitt, *Corpus der italienischen Zeichnungen, 1300–1450*, Berlin, Part I, II, 1968, p. 383ff.

Pp. 126-130 Prato Master, Presentation of the Virgin; Birth of the Virgin; Unbelievers
Mario Salmi, "Paolo Uccello, Domenico Veneziano, Piero della Francesca e gli affreschi del duomo di Prato," *Bollettino d'arte*, XXVIII, 1934–35, pp. 1–16; Pope-Hennessy, *op. cit.*, p. 157ff.; Paolo Dal Poggetto,

in *Catalogue*, p. 144, nos. 34, 35; Giuseppe Marchini, in *Due secoli di pittura murale, mostra di affreschi, sinopie e graffiti dei secoli XIV e XV*, Palazzo Pretorio, Prato, 1969, pp. 66f., 82f., 100f., fig. 13.

P. 132 Domenico Veneziano, John the Baptist and St. Francis

Luciano Berti, in *Mostra di quattro maestri del Primo Rinascimento*, Palazzo Strozzi, Florence, 1954, no. 37, p. 87; Eve Borsook, *The Mural Painters of Tuscany, from Cimabue to Andrea del Sarto*, London, 1960, p. 153f.

Pp. 134, 136 Piero della Francesca, Mary Magdalen

Kenneth Clark, *Piero della Francesca*, London, 1951, p. 41; Roberto Longhi, *Piero della Francesca*, Florence, 1963, p. 55f.

P. 139 Piero della Francesca, The Queen of Sheba

Clark, *op. cit.*, p. 25ff., pl. 39; Longhi, *op. cit.*, pp. 32ff., 82ff., 86, 211, pls. 56, 57.

P. 140 Piero della Francesca, Resurrection

Clark, *op. cit.*, p. 40f.; Longhi, *op. cit.*, p. 53ff.; Creighton Gilbert, *Change in Piero della Francesca*, Locust Valley, N.Y., 1968, pp. 42–45.

P. 145 Piero della Francesca, Dream of Constantine

Clark, *op. cit.*, p. 25f.; Longhi, *op. cit.* pp. 36f., 82ff., 87, 212.

P. 146 Piero della Francesca Workshop, Saint Julian (?)

Mario Salmi, "L'affresco di Sansepolcro," *Bollettino d'arte*, XL, 1955, pp. 230–236; Longhi, *op. cit.*, pp. 168–203; Paolo Dal Poggetto, in *Catalogue*, p. 168, no. 45.

P. 148 Castagno, Cumaean Sibyl

Theodor E. Mommsen, "Petrarch and the Decoration of the Sala Virorum Illustrium in Padua," *Art Bulletin*, XXXIV, 1952, p. 95ff.; Marita Horster, "Castagnos florentiner Fresken 1450–1457," *Wallraf-Richartz Jahrbuch*, XVII, 1955, p. 98ff.; Mario Salmi, *Andrea del Castagno*, Novara, 1961, pp. 26, 48f.

P. 151 Castagno, Resurrection

Mario Salmi, "Nuove rivelazioni su Andrea del Castagno," *Bollettino d'arte*, XXXIX, 1954, p. 29f.; Ugo Procacci, *Sinopie e affreschi*, Milan, 1960, p. 67f., pls. 122–129; Frederick Hartt and Gino Corti, "Andrea del Castagno: Three Disputed Dates," *Art Bulletin*, XLVIII, 1966, p. 228ff.

P. 153 Castagno, Trinity and St. Jerome

Mario Salmi, *Andrea del Castagno*, Novara, 1961, pp. 30f., 50; Millard Meiss, in *Catalogue*, p. 160, nos. 42, 43; Juergen and Anne Markham Schulz, Review of exhibition "The Great Age of Fresco in New York," *Burlington Magazine*, CXI, 1969, p. 51ff.; Frederick Hartt, *History of Italian Renaissance Art*, New York [1969], p. 226. The writer is preparing a study of this painting and the iconography of St. Jerome.

P. 156 Gozzoli, Tabernacle of the Visitation

G. Tosi, "L'edicola 'della Visitazione' presso Castelfiorentino dipinta da Benozzo Gozzoli," *Miscellanea storica della Valdelsa*, V–VI, 1897, pp. 204–216; O. Pogni, "Le iscrizioni di Castelfiorentino," *Miscellanea storica della Valdelsa*, XXV–XXVII, 1917, p. 73f.; Paolo Dal Poggetto, in *Catalogue*, p. 170ff., nos. 46–48.

P. 158 Mantegna, Martyrdom of St. James

Paul Kristeller, *Andrea Mantegna*, London, 1901, p. 104 ff.; Giuseppe Fiocco, *Mantegna. La Cappella Ovetari nella chiesa degli Eremitani*, Milan [1945]; Giovanni Paccagnini, "Cronologia della Cappella Ovetari," in *Atti del VI convegno internazionale di studi sul Rinascimento 1961*, Florence, 1965, pp. 77–85.

Pp. 161, 162 Mantegna, Landscape; Ceiling

Kristeller, *op. cit.*, p. 235ff.; Giovanni Paccagnini, "Appunti sulla tecnica della 'camera picta' di Andrea Mantegna," in *Scritti di storia dell'arte in onore di Mario Salmi*, Rome, II, 1962, pp. 395–403.

P. 164 Cossa, Venus and Her "Children"; Decan

Aby Warburg, *Gesammelte Schriften*, Leipzig, 1932, II, p. 627ff.; J. Seznec, *The Survival of the Pagan Gods*, New York, 1953, p. 207ff.; Paolo d'Ancona, *The Schifanoia Months at Ferrara with a Critical Notice on the Recent Restoration by Cesare Gnudi*, Milan, 1954, p. 35ff.; Roberto Longhi, *Officina ferrarese*, Florence, 1956, p. 30; Eberhard Ruhmer, *Francesco del Cossa*, Munich, 1959, p. 71ff.

P. 169 Ghirlandaio, St. Jerome

Helen I. Robert, "St. Augustine in 'St. Jerome's Study': Carpaccio's Painting and Its Legendary Source," *Art Bulletin*, XLI, 1959, p. 283ff.

P. 170 Botticelli, St. Augustine

Herbert Horne, *Alessandro Filipepi, Commonly Called Sandro Botticelli, Painter of Florence*, London, 1908, p. 66ff.; Robert, *op. cit.*, pp. 238–297.

P. 172   Perugino and Pintoricchio (?), Baptism
Steinmann, *op. cit.*, p. 318 ff.; Ettore Camesasca, *Tutta la pittura del Perugino*, Milan, 1959, p. 53 f., pl. 35; Ettlinger, *op. cit.*, p. 76 f.; Salvini, Camesasca and Ragghianti, *op. cit.*, pp. 40, 148 f., 172 f.

P. 175   Ghirlandaio, Approval of the Franciscan Rule
Aby Warburg, *Gesammelte Schriften*, Leipzig, 1932, I, pp. 97–116; Warman Welliver, "Alterations in Ghirlandaio's S. Trinita Frescoes," *Art Quarterly*, XXXII, 1969, pp. 269–281.

P. 178   Botticelli, The Trials and Triumphs of Moses
Ernst Steinmann, *Die Sixtinische Kapelle*, Munich, I, 1901, p. 262 ff.; Horne, *op. cit.*, p. 100 ff.; Leopold D. Ettlinger, *The Sistine Chapel before Michelangelo. Religious Imagery and Papal Primacy*, Oxford, 1965, pp. 66 ff., 104 ff.; Roberto Salvini, Ettore Camesasca and C. L. Ragghianti, *La Capella Sistina in Vaticano*, Milan [1965], pp. 56 ff., 164 ff.

P. 179   Filippino, Jacob and Abraham
Alfred Scharf, *Filippino Lippi*, Vienna, 1935, pp. 60, 66, 88; Katherine B. Neilson, *Filippino Lippi*, Cambridge, Mass., 1938, p. 159, fig. 78.

P. 183   Signorelli, History of Anti-Christ
Luitpold Dussler, *Signorelli, des Meisters Gemälde*, Stuttgart, 1927, p. xxxiv ff.; Mario Salmi, *Luca Signorelli*, Novara, 1953, p. 24 ff.; André Chastel, *Art et humanisme à Florence au temps de Laurent le Magnifique*, Paris, 1959, p. 444 ff.

P. 184   Fra Bartolommeo, St. Francis Embracing St. Dominic
Guido Carocci, *I dintorni di Firenze*, Florence, I, 1906, p. 174 f.; Hans von der Gabelentz, *Fra Bartolommeo und die florentiner Renaissance*, Leipzig, 1922, I, p. 114, II, pp. 22, 114 f.; Paolo Dal Poggetto, in *Catalogue*, p. 198, no. 55.

P. 185   Sodoma, St. Maurus Treading on Water
Robert H. Cust, *Giovanni Antonio Bazzi*, New York, 1906, pp. 88–106; Enzo Carli, *L'Abbazia di Monteoliveto*, Milan, 1961, p. 39, pl. 43.

P. 188   Michelangelo, Daniel
Charles de Tolnay, *Michelangelo*, Princeton, II, 1945, p. 149; Johannes Wilde, "The Decoration of the Sistine Chapel," *Proceedings of The British Academy*, XLIV, 1958, pp. 61 ff., 78; Herbert von Einem, *Michelangelo*, Stuttgart, 1959, p. 62; Roberto Salvini et al., *La Cappella Sistina in Vaticano*, Milan [1965], p. 209 f.

P. 190   Raphael, Liberation of St. Peter from Prison
Heinrich Wölfflin, *Art of the Italian Renaissance*, New York (n. d.), pp. 158–161; Frederick Hartt, "Lignum Vitae in medio Paradisi," *Art Bulletin*, XXXII, 1950, pp. 121–124; Sydney J. Freedberg, *Painting of the High Renaissance in Rome and Florence*, Cambridge, Mass., 1961, p. 164; John Shearman, "Raphael's Unexecuted Projects for the Stanze," in *Walter Friedlaender zum 90. Geburtstag, eine Festgabe seiner europäischen Schüler, Freunde und Verehrer*, Berlin, 1965, p. 170 ff.; Luitpold Dussler, *Raffael, kritisches Verzeichnis der Gemälde, Wandbilder und Bildteppiche*, Munich, 1966, p. 90 f.

P. 194   Raphael, Galatea
Federico Hermanin, *La Farnesina*, Bergamo, 1927, p. 48 ff.; Arnold von Salis, *Antike und Renaissance*, Zürich, 1947, p. 210 ff.; Lynn White, Jr., *Medieval Technology and Social Change*, Oxford, 1962, p. 114; Ernst Gombrich, *The Story of Art*, London, 1966, p. 234 f.; Dussler, *op. cit.*, p. 109 f. The letter quoted in the text, generally held to have been written by Raphael, has also been ascribed to Pietro Aretino (G. Becatti, in *Raffaelio*, Novara, 1968, p. 530 f.). The writer is preparing a study of Raphael's *Galatea*.

Pp. 197–199   Andrea del Sarto, Feast of Herod; Baptism of the People; The Baptist Preaching
Sydney J. Freedberg, *Andrea del Sarto*, Cambridge, Mass., 1963, pp. 30 f., 32, 35 f., 41 f., 64 f., 66, 70; John Shearman, *Andrea del Sarto*, Oxford, 1965, I, p. 52 ff., II, p. 294 ff.; Paolo Dal Poggetto, in *Catalogue*, p. 200 ff., nos. 58, 59, 63.

P. 200   Pontormo, Madonna and Saints
Frederick M. Clapp, *Jacopo Carucci da Pontormo, His Life and Work*, New Haven, 1916, pp. 7 ff., 15, 117 ff.; Sydney J. Freedberg, *Painting of the High Renaissance in Rome and Florence*, Cambridge, Mass., 1961, p. 245 ff.; Kurt W. Förster, *Pontormo*, Munich, 1966, pp. 20, 128; Luciano Berti, *Pontormo*, Florence, 1964, pp. 36, vi; *idem*, in *Catalogue*, p. 214, no. 66.

P. 202   Pontormo, Annunciation
Clapp, *op. cit.*, pp. 46 ff., 122; Förster, *op. cit.*, pp. 58 ff.,

142 (no. 35), pls. 52, 53, 55, 56; Luciano Berti, *Pontormo*, Florence, 1964, pp. 44, cxf.; *idem*, in *Catalogue*, p. 220, no. 68.

P. 207   Beccafumi, A Roman Tribune Cremates
         His Fellows
Valerius Maximus, *Fatti di Roma* (Collezione di opere inedite o rare dei primi tre secoli della lingua pubblicata per cura della R. Commissione pe' Testi di Lingua nelle prov. dell'Emilia), Bologna, II, 1868, p. 424; Maria Gibellino-Krasceninnicowa, *Il Beccafumi*, Siena, 1933, pp. 76, 176ff.; Aldo Cairola and Enzo Carli, *Il Palazzo Pubblico di Siena*, Rome, 1963, p. 221; Donato Sanminiatelli, *Domenico Beccafumi*, Milan, 1967, pp. 103f., 126, 200, pl. 47.

P. 208   Correggio, Christ and the Apostles
Corrado Ricci, *Antonio Allegri da Correggio*, New York, 1896, p. 197ff.; Augusta Ghidiglia Quintavalle, *Correggio*; *The Frescoes in San Giovanni Evangelista in Parma*, New York, n. d.

P. 211   Michelangelo, Last Judgment
Johannes Wilde, "The Decoration of the Sistine Chapel," *Proceedings of The British Academy*, XLIV, 1958, p. 78f.; Herbert von Einem, *Michelangelo*, Stuttgart, 1959, p. 113ff.; Charles de Tolnay, *Michelangelo*, Princeton, V, 1960, p. 19ff.; Deoclecio Redig de Campos, *Il Giudizio universale di Michelangelo*, Milan, 1964; Roberto Salvini, Ettore Camesasca and C.L. Ragghianti, *La Cappella Sistina in Vaticano*, Milan [1965], pp. 103ff., 224ff.; Frederick Hartt, *History of Italian Renaissance Art*, New York [1969], p. 574ff.

P. 213   Bronzino, The Miraculous Spring of
         Moses
Arthur McComb, *Agnolo Bronzino, His Life and Works*, Cambridge, Mass., 1928, pp. 33f., 56; Andrea Emiliani, *Il Bronzino*, Busto Arsizio, 1960, p. 66f., pl. 45, and text to pls. 33–36.

P. 214   Allori, Trinity
Hans Geisenheimer, "Di alcune pitture fiorentine eseguite intorno al 1570," *Arte e storia*, XXVI, 1907, p. 19ff.; Umberto Baldini, in *Catalogue*, p. 228ff.; David Summers, "The Sculptural Program of the Cappella di San Luca in the Santissima Annunziata," *Mitteilungen des Kunsthistorischen Institutes in Florenz*, XL, 1969, p. 67ff.

P. 216   Titian, Landscape (Detail)
Hans Tietze, *Titian. Paintings and Drawings*, New York, 1950, p. 9f.; Francesco Valcanover, *All the Paintings of Titian*, London, 1965, I, pp. 14, 52, pls. 30, 31.

Pp. 218–223   Veronese, Salone; Sala della Lu-
         cerna; Landscape, Sala dell'Olimpo
Rodolfo Pallucchini and Alba Medea, in *Palladio, Veronese e Vittoria a Maser*, Milan, 1960, pp. 69ff., 89ff., 127ff., 143ff.; A. Richard Turner, *The Vision of Landscape in Renaissance Italy*, Princeton, 1966, p. 208ff.; Juergen Schulz, "Le fonti di Paolo Veronese come decoratore," *Bollettino del Centro internazionale di studi d'architettura A. Palladio*, X, 1968, p. 241ff.

P. 224   Carracci, Ceiling, Farnese Gallery
Rudolf Wittkower, *Art and Architecture in Italy 1600–1750*, Harmondsworth, 1958, p. 36ff.; John R. Martin, *The Farnese Gallery*, Princeton, 1965, pp. 52ff., 83ff., 190ff.; Charles Dempsey, "'Et nos cedamus amori': Observations on the Farnese Gallery," *Art Bulletin*, L, 1968, pp. 363–374.

P. 226   Pietro da Cortona, The Age of Gold
Giuliano Briganti, *Pietro da Cortona o della pittura Barocca*, Florence, 1962, pp. 95, 215; Malcolm Campbell, Letter in *Burlington Magazine*, CIV, 1962, p. 121ff.; *idem*, "Medici Patronage and the Baroque," *Art Bulletin*, XLVIII, 1966, pp. 133–141.

P. 228   Tiepolo, The Angel Rescues Hagar and
         Ishmael; Sacrifice of Isaac
Antonio Morassi, *G. B. Tiepolo: His Life and Work*, London, 1955, pp. 12, 143; *idem*, *A Complete Catalogue of the Paintings of G. B. Tiepolo*, London, 1962, pp. 53, 230.

INDEX

Detached frescoes are indexed with the buildings for which they were painted even though they may not yet have been returned to these buildings. Page numbers in italics refer to illustration pages.

SOURCES OF ILLUSTRATIONS

Lee Boltin: 32, 57 (left), 59, 61, 81, 104, 108, 120, 129, 147, 152, 154, 155, 157, 196, 199, 201, 205

Camposanto Monumentale in Pisa, Opera della Primaziale Pisana, 1960, pl. 17: 89

Alfio del Serra: 33

Foto Zenit Color, Pistoia: 82

Frank Malfara: 22

Mantegna. La Cappella Ovetari nella Chiesa degli Eremitani, Collezione Silvana, Monumenti della Civiltà Pittorica Italiana, 1945, pl. 9: 159

Metropolitan Museum of Art, New York: 26

Piero della Francesca, *De prospectiva pingendi*, ed. G. Nicco Fasola, Florence, n. d., pl. 37: 136

Fulvio Roiter, 219, 221, 223

Giuseppe Rosi: 126

Scala Istituto Fotografico Editoriale, Florence: 25, 29, 31, 35, 36, 39, 41, 43, 44, 47, 49, 51, 53, 54, 57 (right), 62–63, 64, 65, 67, 68, 71, 73, 74, 76, 79, 80, 83, 85, 86, 87, 90, 91, 93, 94, 96, 99, 101, 103, 105, 109, 110, 111, 112, 115, 116, 118, 121, 122, 124, 125, 127, 131, 133, 135, 137, 138, 141, 143, 144, 149, 150, 160, 161, 163, 165, 166–167, 168, 171, 173, 174, 176–177, 180, 181, 182, 184, 186–187, 189, 192–193, 195, 198, 203, 206, 209, 210, 212, 215, 217, 225, 227, 229, 230–231

Soprintendenza alle Gallerie, Gabinetto Fotografico, Florence: 19

Leonetto Tintori: 9, 17